THE MIND'S EAR

PRAISE FOR THE SECOND EDITION

I have known Bruce Adolphe since my student days at Juilliard Pre-College. His insight and remarkable capacity for bringing music to life have stayed with me over the years. Bruce's ability to make music and learning fresh and alive is unique. The first edition of this book was important to me when I first read it and the second edition is even more exciting and relevant.

—ALAN GILBERT, *music director, The New York Philharmonic*

Imagine how exciting it would be to hold in your hands a guide to a more joyfully free, creative engagement with music. Oh wait—you are! Of course the imagination can be toned and exercised, and Bruce Adolphe is a most enthusiastic and inspiring personal trainer.

—MARK STEINBERG, *violinist, Brentano String Quartet, Princeton University*

Long known as one of our most articulate and charismatic speakers on music, Bruce Adolphe here gives us one of the freshest books on the musical imagination ever written. A quick glance at the materials followed by a self-test will confirm that the mature performer and the university professor have as much to learn from this book as the beginner. The book is an absolute gem, one that I periodically find myself opening at random as a starting point for pricking the imagination. Try opening it yourself, and I predict that you will find it difficult to put down.

—GLENN WATKINS, *Earl V. Moore Professor Emeritus, University of Michigan, author of Soundings; Pyramids at the Louvre; Proof through the Night: Music and the Great War; and The Gesualdo Hex*

Bruce Adolphe's Senior Seminar at Juilliard's Pre-College was a horizon-expanding, mind-broadening experience. This book contains dozens of exercises like the ones we used in that class. I find them just as rewarding today as I did then!

—ORLI SHAHAM, *pianist*

This unique book of musical imagination exercises is thoroughly infused with Bruce Adolphe's engaging spirit and personality. Dozens of exercises inspire creativity and exploration while probing the depths of our inner ears and our intuition. I believe this is an invaluable resource for all musicians, pedagogues and listeners.

—CAROL LEONE, D.M.A., *chair of the Keyboard Department, associate professor of piano, Meadows School of the Arts, Southern Methodist University, Dallas, Texas*

I often tell conducting students that the greatest conductors are those with the greatest imaginations. They hear in their minds what they would like the music to become and are tenacious and creative in making it happen. Bruce Adolphe's wonderful book presents tools to develop the artistic imagination. If technique is the servant of imagination, then Adolphe's book is the place to start!

—JERRY BLACKSTONE, *professor of conducting; director of choirs; chair, Conducting Department, School of Music, Theatre and Dance, University of Michigan*

THIRD EDITION

THE MIND'S EAR

*Exercises for Improving the Musical
Imagination for Performers,
Composers, and Listeners*

BRUCE ADOLPHE

OXFORD
UNIVERSITY PRESS

OXFORD
UNIVERSITY PRESS

Oxford University Press is a department of the University of Oxford. It furthers the University's objective of excellence in research, scholarship, and education by publishing worldwide. Oxford is a registered trade mark of Oxford University Press in the UK and certain other countries.

Published in the United States of America by Oxford University Press
198 Madison Avenue, New York, NY 10016, United States of America.

Library of Congress Control Number: 2021940511
ISBN 978-0-19-757632-8 (pbk.)
ISBN 978-0-19-757631-1 (hbk.)

DOI: 10.1093/oso/9780197576311.001.0001

Hardback printed by Bridgeport National Bindery, Inc., United States of America

The original exercises were developed at The Juilliard School Pre-College Division Senior Seminar and the Performance Awareness Workshops at the Chamber Music Society of Lincoln Center.

The book is dedicated to my many students over many years—at Juilliard, Yale, New York University, the Chamber Music Society of Lincoln Center, and at colleges and festivals too many to mention; to my friends at the Kinhaven Music School, where I was greatly inspired as a teenager; to Linda Granitto, who was director of the Juilliard Pre-College Division when the exercises were first developed; and of course, to my wife, Marija Stroke, and our daughter, Katja Stroke-Adolphe, both of whom have wonderful imaginations.

CONTENTS

ABOUT THE THIRD EDITION

The first edition of *The Mind's Ear: Exercises for Improving the Musical Imagination for Performers, Composers, and Listeners* was a small handbook of 40 exercises published in 1991 by MMB Music, Inc., which was my music publisher at the time. The exercises and games in that first volume were the consequence of my theater-game-inspired experiments with my students at the Juilliard Pre-College, where I taught from 1974 to 1993. During part of that period, I was not only teaching solfège, theory, and composition but also composing music for plays presented by the Juilliard Drama Division. My ongoing work with the Drama faculty resulted in frequent invitations to audit acting classes, which had an enormous impact on the central idea of this book.

Suzanne Ryan, then Editor in Chief, Humanities, at Oxford University Press, invited me to create a much expanded and revised second edition, which was published in 2013. For that edition, I doubled the number of exercises and wrote a series of essays about the musical imagination and about various methods of unleashing creativity.

This third edition, written in response to the kind invitation of Oxford's Michelle Chen and Norman Hirschy, includes
34 new exercises created to further explore concepts that inspire imaginative musicianship for performers, composers,
and listeners through improvisations based on theater games,
comedy improv methods, and the interplay of verbal and non-
verbal thinking.

One aspect of *The Mind's Ear* that has made it accessible and
useful in varied educational situations from elementary schools
to university music departments and conservatories is that the
majority of the exercises/games are performable at any level of
musical competence and experience, and in any musical style.
Many of the improvisations do not specify any stylistic orienta-
tion or require a particular musical vocabulary, but rather focus
on dramatic situations, emotional qualities, actions, and goals.
This freedom from technical restrictions is an approach drawn
from the theater world. Some of the exercises in this book do require familiarity with particular styles, sometimes introducing
specific composers or performers, yet even these exercises offer
a wide range of possibilities for students of varied experience.

My own musical background and professional life have been
formed principally by the European Classical tradition, but my
work is also richly informed by American popular songs, jazz
music, and folk music from around the world, which I learned
growing up because my parents were avid folk-dancers and
teachers with a sizable collection of recordings.

At its best, music education is an invitation to experience
music and to discover one's own musical imagination. While
musicians in music departments and conservatories will naturally adapt the exercises here to suit their specific musical
pursuits, the material in this book is also useful for general
music education. Inclusivity and diversity are essential aspects
of a meaningful modern music education environment and
those principles significantly inform the learning strategies in

this book. Music education should not be an indoctrination into an established hierarchy of humanity's achievements, reflecting the underlying power structure of society, telling students what is great and must be appreciated. Rather, a student whose imagination is awakened through firsthand experience with music and whose own culture is accepted and embraced by these experiences will naturally come to hear all kinds of music as her own to enjoy, perform, and compose. A genuine love of music is more than an appreciation of it.

These exercises may be used in very different circumstances: a community workshop where musicians of different levels and musical styles work together; chamber ensemble classes at a conservatory; solfège and ear-training class; theory class; imagination masterclasses for one instrument (violin class, piano class, etc.); composition class or private lessons (in any style); a general music education class where certain of these exercises (*Exercises to Be Done in Silence* and *Exercises Involving Groups*) may enhance or replace standard appreciation courses; audience workshops to explore listening skills (same two chapters); group activities at music conferences; and all but the group exercises are designed so that they may be used by one person alone.

The Mind's Ear approach, like the theater games it is inspired by, focuses on imagination, expressivity, openness, and playfulness. An improvisation leader or music instructor can use these exercises to explore jazz, classical, pop, world music, or even a non-defined style, one that is freeform and eclectic and that evolves in the moment. One central goal in all the editions of *The Mind's Ear* is the concept that "technique" is not only a matter of physical dexterity, but it is first and foremost the ability to communicate and project a musical idea, to let the music speak.

Another essential concept of *The Mind's Ear* is that the exploratory process is the point. These exercises are not meant as a means for assessment and they are not about right and wrong. They are about experimenting with music in a spirit of playfulness. The teacher, if there is one, is not there to give approval or disapproval, but rather to encourage, guide, question, challenge, and enjoy the learning process. If a student is stuck during an exercise, the leader or teacher might ask, "What if . . ." What if this chord (or this note, or this rhythm, etc.) suddenly entered the musical scenario? What if you played like you have a sugar buzz or you just won the lottery? What if you know that if you stop playing you will be attacked by a grizzly bear? What if there were no tests, no grades, no reviews?

The Mind's Ear provides portals to creativity. The exercises encourage musicians to react intuitively to varied dramatic and emotional situations, to play spontaneously, to be in the moment, to shake free of stale conventions, and to find personal ways to be inspired easily and often. The ultimate goal is for musicians—performers and composers—to be truly themselves in their music-making.

The third edition has 34 new exercises, 14 of which are based on concepts related to my piano puzzlers on public radio.

Some new ideas that appear in this third edition are exercises inspired by improv comedy (see the *Nichols and May* exercises), hip-hop (see *Sample Sale*), robots (see *Roboto/Rubato* and *Remote Control*), and more of my personal experiences in theater (see *Street Scene*).

There is a brand-new section at the end of the third edition called *Piano Puzzler Preparation*. I have been performing my piano puzzlers on public radio's *Performance Today*, hosted by Fred Child, since 2002. As I write this, there are about 600 piano puzzlers in my computer. What is a piano puzzler? The recipe is to take a familiar tune (a popular song, folk song, show tune, children's song, or tune from any other genre) and recompose it in the style of a famous classical composer, perhaps using an actual piece by that composer as the foundation of the puzzler. The composers whose styles and pieces I have used to create the puzzlers include Handel, Bach, Scarlatti, Haydn, Mozart, Beethoven, Schubert, Mendelssohn, Chopin, Wagner, Liszt, Brahms, Dvořák, Janáček, Fauré, Mussorgsky, Debussy, Ravel, Puccini, Satie, Schoenberg, Berg, Stravinsky, Prokofiev, Bartók, Messiaen, Poulenc, Shostakovich, Britten, and Copland. While the tunes range across genres and include many folk songs from around the world, the majority of the popular songs are by Kern, Gershwin, Arlen, Berlin, Rodgers, Porter, Weill, and the Beatles.

The exercises in the *Piano Puzzler Preparation* section require keyboard skills and a knowledge of harmony—plus having some experience composing definitely helps. I have included this rather challenging section in the book because pianists, piano teachers, and composers around the United States, including teachers who have used *The Mind's Ear*, have told me that they have found the piano puzzlers to be good teaching tools and that they would love to have a resource to help them use the puzzlers with their students. So, styled in the manner of *The Mind's Ear* exercises using both improvisation and composition, the third edition provides that resource.

PREFACE

A good technique serves the imagination

The exercises in this book cover a wide range of techniques and approaches to engaging the musical imagination, including suggestions for imagining music in silence that one may do alone, performance games for the solo player, group games with and without instruments, games involving a wide variety of improvisation procedures, and experiments in musical imagining that involve composing. The exercises can be used by a wide variety of readers: the interested listener; students in an introductory music appreciation class; music performance classes from elementary to high school; and conservatory students, including the most advanced. Even many professional musicians I know, some of whom have very active international careers in chamber music and as soloists, have told me that they have found the imagination exercises stimulating, fun to do, and inspiring. I like doing them myself, I admit!

The idea that something important was missing in music education first occurred to me after an incident in one of my classes at the Juilliard Pre-College Division where I taught from 1974 to 1993. I had asked the students to harmonize a melody that was written on the chalkboard. These students were a motivated group, all proficient instrumentalists with a lively interest in the work we did in theory class, and yet they seemed to be silently struggling with this assignment. A hand went up, followed by the question, "Are we allowed to use the piano to work on this?" I replied, "Just hear it in your head. Use harmonies you know." The student answered, "I don't really hear anything when I can't use an instrument."

I had the feeling I needed to explore this problem, as it was probably typical and usually ignored. "Do you mean you can't hear triads and seventh chords in your mind?" He was a student whose theory work on paper was always excellent. He answered, "Not really. I just know what works and I recognize it as right or wrong only after I hear it or sing it." When I had played chords of various types on the piano for this class, they had little trouble identifying the harmonies. But that was reactive, not creative. And yet, I thought, they must have clear sonic memories of these harmonies, accurate sound images that they can summon to be able to recognize the chords when they are actually played. So I asked the whole group, "How many of you can look at music printed on a page and hear it in your minds without using an instrument?"

Only one hand went up; then it went down. None of them felt sure that they could hear in silence, in the mind's ear. Even students with perfect pitch felt the need to sing or play the music out loud to be sure of their work on paper. When I gave these students a page of printed music to follow as I played for them at the piano, they could easily catch a wrong note planted for them as a test, no matter how subtle. And yet hearing in silence was somehow an elusive art. Feeling challenged to deal with this, I said, "Put your papers away and listen—try to hear what I describe. Hear in your mind a major scale played loudly on a piano." (I did not touch the keyboard.) "Now hear it played on a violin." (The room was completely silent. I waited and watched their faces, which told of real effort and genuine interest.) "Now hear each note played on a different instrument: piano, violin, clarinet, oboe, horn, flute, trumpet, vibraphone."

Some of the students found this rather difficult while others became very excited because the sounds were becoming real in their minds, the suggestion of different timbres adding a level of reality to the exercise. These preliminary exercises evolved in theory and solfège classes, and this led to the organization of a special seminar devoted to the imagination. Eventually, the idea of musical suggestions for the "mind's ear" was expanded to include emotional and dramatic suggestions to inspire more imaginative performances, and these exercises were soon combined with theater games and experiments in improvisation and composition. The first edition of this book emerged as a guide to what we did in this seminar.

The second edition of *The Mind's Ear* included all the original exercises from the first edition, some of which had been revised and expanded, plus many brand-new exercises that I had tried with students at high schools, colleges, and conservatories across the country since the first edition was published. This third edition, as described above, expands the book once again.

A NOTE TO TEACHERS (AND
STUDENTS, TOO)

1. Imagine you are in the audience at a concert: the lights dim—soon a violinist walks on stage and begins to play a wild, thrilling kind of music for solo violin. The music pulsates, the rhythms shifting unpredictably, and then it soars into the upper register. Suddenly there is brief silence, and then a quiet, gentle melody on the G-string appears, hovers in the air, and finally fades into a longer silence. It is over. You love the music, rise to your feet with the rest of the audience, and shout, "Bravo!" Can you remember what you heard? Describe it or play it on the piano. Try to write some of it down.

2. Imagine you are in the audience of a courtroom trial. A man who has just been wrongly convicted of a serious crime suddenly turns to the jury and makes an impassioned speech, trying to convince them of his innocence. His voice rises higher and higher until he is screaming at them, and then suddenly he collapses and

is silent. The court is stunned. The man stands up and quietly asks for their mercy and understanding. No one speaks. Take this scene and use it to create a short violin solo.

3. Assignment: Write a short work for solo violin with changing meters and accents. Be sure to use the entire range of the instrument and include some mood changes.

The three paragraphs above present three perspectives on the same unwritten music and demonstrate three ways to give an assignment to a composition student or theory class.

The first paragraph asks you to imagine music you have never heard as if you were an excited audience member, thrilled by what you hear. The music is described emotionally with some basic musical suggestions to guide the imagination. Because you are asked to imagine this musical scene as an audience member, you feel as though you are in a theater listening, and you are neither the performer nor the composer of the work. Your imagination is set free.

The second approach does not mention music at all, but rather presents a human drama that could be interpreted musically. Your compassion for the character and your sense of drama is engaged, and it is likely that you will compose with passion and a sense of mission. It is an important aspect of this scenario that there are no details. We do not know the nature of the crime or any aspect of the situation; we do not know what the evidence is, why the jury convicted him, or what he says to them. In fact, because we know the feelings and the structure but not the details of the scenario, the scene is very much like music.

The third is a typical school assignment—dull, uninspiring, constraining, and hard to do.

Yet all three are the same assignment. The point is clear: the way we teach can inspire creativity or dull it. The assignment in the third paragraph is hard to do because it does not provide motivation. Why use changing meters? Why shifting accents? What is the point of using the entire range of the instrument? The only reason here is the implied testing of skill. This is no fun. It is not an artistic assignment. Technique is best taught as a means to expression within a context.

I am convinced that most people know why they love music and want to study it, but in the study of the techniques of the art it is easy to lose sight of the why. The way to teach music, to my way of thinking, is to remember at all times that technique is not a goal but the means to the goal. Technique exists only to serve music, and techniques have evolved and changed in order to express new ideas in music. Of course, sometimes it is necessary to isolate a technical problem in order to solve it, to work it through, but even then it is better to link it to a musical thought than to let the technical problem become "the point."

How is technique in composition to be differentiated from music theory—or, to put it differently, how is creativity to be distinguished from musical competency? This is simple: in a music theory assignment, the goal is to demonstrate an understanding of the material; but in a composition assignment, the goal is to express an idea with clarity. Taking this further, it is vital that a composition student be emotionally engaged with every phrase, to be excited by every choice made. I tell my students only to show me work that they love—if they are not happy with music they have written, they should keep working on it. If they are not happy with the music, they probably know why, too. There is a famous story of Mendelssohn becoming enraged (very unusual for him) with one of his composition students because the student titled his piece "Charivari"—and Mendelssohn told him, "If you think it is rubbish, why should

I waste my time with it?" (He analyzed it anyway, because he could not resist.)

One way to encourage creative thinking in written musical assignments is to suggest that students try the opposite of whatever is comfortable to do. For example, if it seems easier for students to write a melody and then compose harmony for it, suggest composing the harmonies first, and the melody after.

For students who must write at a piano, suggest writing at a desk without the aid of an instrument. But if a student always writes at a desk and is uncomfortable improvising at the piano, improvisation should be prescribed. These suggestions are not meant to be corrections, nor are they supposed to be permanent—they are not even improvements. They are challenges. Such challenges stimulate new responses, get the mind working differently, and so open up new channels for creativity.

Just as the opening three exercises demonstrate the importance of engaging the emotions when addressing technique, it is helpful to look at all music as part of a larger context, to relate it to the wider world. The study of fugue, canon, sonata, and other compositional traditions should be more than exercises in thematic imitation, transposition, development, and variation—but also a study of worldviews. For example, we should ask, "What did canon mean in the Baroque period? How did Bach understand counterpoint in terms of his view of the divine, of the universe, of nature? What essential idea is communicated by the floating harmonies of Debussy that is different from the functional progressions in Beethoven?" Technique should be tied to meaning.

When I was a student at Juilliard, I studied canon writing—including double canons, inversion canon, and other canon types but I didn't think that I would actually use those techniques in my own music. I enjoyed the intricacy of these old-fashioned techniques, but thought that canons were of little use to me personally. But then, years later, when composing a work in which I wanted to express the despair of a person who was suffering from cancer, I found that a double canon provided me with a structure that by its very nature was about the struggle between destiny and free will. A canon has laws that make it what it is, and the music must unfold according to those laws (destiny), yet the composer makes decisions that make the canon unique (free will). When the expressive need arose, I discovered that an ancient technique served well.

Since that time, I have written many pieces in which I needed compositional techniques that could communicate extramusical concepts. For example, in two of my compositions based on neuroscience, I developed musical parallels to biological processes in the brain. The two works—*Memories of a Possible Future* and *Self Comes to Mind*—are both based on writings by neuroscientist Antonio Damasio. For the first work, I used neurobiological concepts in Damasio's book *Descartes' Error*, and for *Self Comes to Mind*, Damasio wrote a text specifically for me to interpret musically. My desire to find musical means to express scientific ideas opened up a new world of compositional processes for me personally. I strongly recommend the exploration of disciplines outside the world of music as a way to spark the imagination.

One last assignment: Imagine you are in a classroom where you can ask students to close their eyes and imagine music they have never heard, a classroom where you can encourage students to let their minds wander, and where you help them follow their thoughts, you help them remember these musical daydreams, and you ask them to describe what they heard, to write it down in words, perhaps in musical notation. And you do not have to test them. Imagine that!

A WORD ABOUT IMPROVISATION FOR

CLASSICAL MUSICIANS

Classical musicians are likely to be familiar with the expression "don't look at the rearview mirror while you're driving," meaning that if you are performing (especially from memory) and you make a mistake, *don't dwell on it*—it's in the past and you are moving forward. This is good advice. But when you are improvising, "looking through the rearview mirror" is a good idea.

During an improvisation, you must keep in mind what you have played and, unlike in a performance of a composed work, you do not really know where you are going! By holding musical ideas in the mind—being attentive to fleeting moments, remembering one-off gestures, and recalling flashes of inspiration—an improviser can create a sustained and cohesive musical experience. When a performer brings back an idea that had emerged spontaneously earlier in the improvisation, the music takes on a feeling of form and a sense of purpose, bringing the listener along in an increasingly comprehensible narrative. The more an improviser can remember what has already happened, the more successfully she can develop a sense of musical architecture.

HOW TO USE THIS BOOK

Anyone interested in developing the ability to hear music in the mind can do the exercises designed to be done in silence, in the mind's ear. You may find that these exercises can help pass the time creatively and constructively on buses, trains, and planes; in doctor's waiting rooms; and just about anywhere you can concentrate. (They will do more for your creativity and listening skills than searching for information on your smart phone.) Some of these exercises "in silence" require no musical training. However, most of the exercises in the book do require a basic knowledge of music, including familiarity with the timbres of musical instruments and a rudimentary understanding of scales and harmony. Some exercises require more advanced skills in performance or composition. Musicians should try all the exercises, even those that seem to require no musical knowledge or experience, because these exercises can help enliven the aural imagination in important ways. These exercises may be done in a classroom, in a chamber music setting, with a group of friends, or even in a preconcert setting with a willing audience, and in such cases a teacher or leader should read the exercises aloud and guide the listeners through the experience, giving them time to imagine each suggestion before moving on. It is also beneficial to follow up with a discussion among the participants. *The Mind's Ear* website gives examples of real sounds to give some perspective to the experience of imagining in silence.

The exercises that require performance on musical instruments may be done with or without a teacher or leader present. In a music class, a teacher who has selected the best exercises for a particular group of music students should feel free to experiment with the exercise, to take it further, or cut it short depending on the situation. It is always a good idea to give the students time to find their way in any exercise, to try it more than once, and to come back to the exercise another day, after having tried some of the other games in the book. Returning to a favorite exercise regularly, perhaps once a week as a standard warm-up for class, can lead to remarkable improvements and a sense of ease with a formerly challenging task. Another good way to involve a group of music students is to let one of the students be the leader of one of the improvisations, and for the teacher to sit back and observe.

The compositional exercises in this book are meant for everyone who has an itch to try composing. While students with compositional experience and advanced theory students may be the obvious candidates for many of these exercises, every musician should try composing and will find these exercises fun to do. One of the main goals of this book is to break down the barriers that prevent some musicians from improvising and composing, to make it fun to engage in creative exploration. Musical examples within the book offer possible "solutions" to some of these compositional exercises. Most of the exercises, however, are left for the reader to explore without examples, so that the imagination is not overly influenced by my particular solutions.

MORE TIPS FOR USING THIS BOOK

The exercises in this book may be used in a variety of ways, including:

1. Warm-ups for a performance class (use the exercises "to be done in the mind" to wake up the imagination and have some fun as a group before rehearsal).

2. As a break from rehearsing repertoire, the improvisation exercises (using instruments) can help free the mind, ease performance nerves, and let people get to know each other in a new way.

3. As an introduction to theory or composition classes, any exercise in the book (and especially the composition and piano puzzler exercises) offers a fun way to explore "technique" and encourage group/class interaction.

4. For an instrumental class (such as a piano masterclass) before and after focusing on repertoire. This offers a break from traditional (and often stressful) masterclass performances and critiques and allows the group to have some fun while exploring imaginative paths to artistic expression.

5. As homework or in regular practicing routines: Encourage students to try some of the improvisations every day as part of practicing, perhaps to start a practice session, as a break in the middle of the practice session, or as a fun coda at the end of the session. If students are willing, they could video their improvisations and show them in class. (No grades!)

6. For team teaching: What if several teachers got together with all their students once in a while and used these exercises as a way for everyone to unleash some creative energy and explore musical expression? It is a good way to break barriers and build some comradery.

7. Teaching online? These games and exercises work on Zoom, or any similar platform, without compromise. In addition to imagination games, there are improvisations that can be done without instruments, as well as solo instrumental improvisations that each class member can try, while the rest of the class listens and reacts. For a while, perhaps for half of every Zoom session, we can forget our instruments and repertoire and concentrate on exploring our musical imaginations and accessing our emotions.

WHAT LEVEL OF MUSICIANSHIP IS REQUIRED FOR THE EXERCISES?

If you understand the terminology in the description of an exercise, try it! Every exercise may be attempted by anyone willing to do so, and there will be surprises for the teachers and students alike. If I were to label an exercise as "beginner" or "advanced" it would create a mindset that inhibits creativity and impedes full engagement with the task. I have been amazed by young, inexperienced students doing supposedly "advanced" exercises beautifully and intuitively, and I have been equally delighted by watching professional musicians thoroughly enjoy exploring a simple suggestion in the book. The most effective way to use this book is to let go of hierarchies and expectations and to be open to surprise.

The new *Piano Puzzler Preparation* section of the book is addressed specifically to pianists and typically requires some knowledge of modes, harmony, and other compositional vocabularies. However, if a violinist wants to adapt one of the exercises to violin and approaches it intuitively or "by ear," that is wonderful, too. I have seen many musicians who profess to know "no theory" demonstrate a depth of compositional understanding when they play by ear "without thinking" about it. This is to be encouraged. The mind's ear is both conscious and subconscious.

What about lesson plans? I suggest that teachers read through the exercises and select just one or two that they feel might work with their students. Try one exercise every day for one week and see how it develops. If it is not evolving and the students are not fully engaged, switch to another exercise. It is a good policy to use an exercise regularly so that students begin to get the feel of it, so they are comfortable and can see each other improve.

The Mind's Ear is a resource book, not a step-by-step series of exercises that need to be done in a certain order, and there is certainly no need to try them all. We all learn best when we are inspired and having fun, and with that in mind, think of *The Mind's Ear* as a stash of games that you found in the attic. Pull one out and try it. Too hard or not your thing exactly? No problem, try another game. Every time someone tries one of these exercises, the result is unique.

LIST OF EXERCISES

I. EXERCISES TO BE DONE IN SILENCE

II. EXERCISES INVOLVING GROUPS

III. EXERCISES USING MUSICAL INSTRUMENTS

IV. THE FEELING OF AN IDEA

V. EXERCISES IN COMPOSING

VI. PIANO PUZZLER PREPARATION

VI. PIANO PUZZLES OR PREPARATION

ABOUT THE COMPANION WEBSITE

www.oup.com/us/themindsear

Oxford has created a companion website to accompany *The Mind's Ear* which has been updated for the third edition. The principal aim of the website is to provide the reader with instructive and inspiring video examples of some of the improvisation and composition exercises in the book. The reader should not *imitate* the demonstrations on the website, but rather use them as a guide to explore his/her own musical thoughts. All the improvisation examples on the website are truly spontaneous improvisations, filmed without any predetermined material or rehearsal and without any editing. In addition to the improvisation videos, the musical examples printed in the book are available on this website. The revamped website also includes new audio clips showcasing performances of piano puzzlers as well as a behind-the-scenes look at the process of creating a piano puzzler.

The performers on the website are violinists Nicolas Kendall and Katja Stroke-Adolphe (age 14 when this was recorded) and cellists Mike Block and Nicholas Canellakis. The pianists featured are Fabio Luisi, Orli Shaham, Joseph Kalichstein, Marija Stroke, Orion Weiss, and the book's author, Bruce Adolphe. The videos on the website were produced by Tristan Cooke with the exception of the piano puzzler video, recorded by the author in his studio in December, 2020.

Online examples are signaled with Oxford's symbol ⬤.

INTRODUCTION

Performers and the Imagination

> I don't play accurately—anyone can play accurately—
> but I play with wonderful expression. As far as the
> piano is concerned, sentiment is my forte. I keep sci-
> ence for life.
>
> —OSCAR WILDE, *The Importance of Being Earnest*

HAVE YOU EVER heard a pianist who was "all fingers and no soul," as the saying goes?

At conservatories and music departments, young musicians are taught technique. That is, they are taught the mechanics of instrumental playing and usually learn phrasing and style by practicing pieces. Technique is extremely important. Without a solid technique, a musician cannot begin to realize her own musical ideas or communicate a piece to an audience. Typically, it is expected that a student's interpretive powers deepen as more and more music is practiced and performed, and through coaching and chamber music experience. Certainly, for many very talented young musicians, this works very well. But what about those who need something more, whose musical imaginations are not engaged by the routine of practicing for hours a day? Can something be done to unleash the musical imagination, to help a young performer "open up" emotionally? Some would say that not everything can be taught and that a student

The Mind's Ear. Bruce Adolphe, Oxford University Press. © Oxford University Press 2021.
DOI: 10.1093/oso/9780197576311.003.0001

is either imaginative or not, emotional or not, talented or not, and that the musical imagination will blossom of its own accord.

During many years of teaching at Juilliard, Yale, the Chamber Music Society of Lincoln Center, and at music departments and festivals around the United States, I have learned that it is most definitely possible to stimulate and enliven students' imaginations through emotionally and intellectually engaging exercises. We must face the fact that the creative energy of many young performing musicians is not fully nourished by practicing, performing, and the conventional theory and solfège classes.

The musical imagination and the mind's ear can be improved by practicing the appropriate exercises, just as is typically done with instrumental technique. The primary goal of developing the mind's ear is to improve the ability to imagine and remember music, to hear music in silence, and to be able to hear in the mind music that is printed on the page without the aid of instrument. Another benefit of this skill is the ability to imagine how one might play a phrase before physically trying to do so on an instrument. This is essential to freeing oneself from habits and discovering deeper levels of interpretation as a performer. While some musicians do this quite naturally, those who find it difficult can work on it and learn to do it well. The exercises in this book are designed to provoke and challenge the mind, and to develop the mind's ear.

Equally important is the ability to bring authentic emotions into play during performance. This is not the same as imitating the emotional posture of one's teacher or favorite artist, nor is it the same as "indicating" emotions by employing clichéd physical gestures, whether or not they are deliberate or unconscious. How do you get a young violinist who is technically capable of playing a difficult concerto but who does not seem to be communicating the music emotionally to be genuinely expressive, to connect more deeply with the essence of the music? For the answer to this problem, I turned to the techniques used to train actors.

I have based my approach to this issue to a great extent on the theater games that are so familiar to drama students but generally are unknown to music students and to most music teachers as well. My inspiration has been the work of Stanislavsky, Stella Adler, Lee Strasberg, Jerzy Grotowski, and others who have brought vitality and technique to the training of actors, helping them to get in touch with their emotions, stimulate their memories, and free their imaginations. My work with drama students at New York University's Tisch School of the Arts from 1984 to 1993 was synthesized with my experiences teaching composition, theory, and solfège at Juilliard to produce this approach to training the musical imagination.

Practicing for three or more hours a day, as many musicians do, will not produce a mature performer unless the musical inner life is also addressed. Strengthening emotional memory, imagination, and the mind's ear can lead to more meaningful interpretations, more communicative performances, and even shave off a few hours of learning-by-rote time.

Some of these exercises may seem extremely simple at first. Do not be fooled. It is important to warm up the imagination just as you would your voice before singing or your limbs before dancing. Any good musician knows that to play scales and arpeggios beautifully is not at all easy, just as a good dancer or athlete knows the difficulties of moving efficiently. If you come back to the more basic, introductory exercises after doing the advanced ones, you may find that the simpler exercises now seem to offer a new experience, a deeper level of awareness.

And yes, do try this at home!

SOMETHING TO SAY

A common criticism of a new work—whether it is a musical composition, dance, play, or painting—is, "It was well crafted, but I don't think the composer (or author, etc.) had anything to say." This reproach is also used to dismiss a performance when the listener feels that the player was emotionally unsatisfying.

Is there really anyone who has nothing to say? A colleague of mine at NYU, where I taught in the drama department in the 1980s and early 1990s, was teaching a course in comedy writing. After giving a demonstration to his new class by telling some stories of his childhood that had the class in stitches, he overheard a student say, "It's no fair, his life was really funny."

We all have plenty to say if only we can learn to explore our memories and let our imaginations go. Our education, musical and otherwise, can and should encourage self-exploration as a path to understanding others and also as a way to free our imaginations for creative work.

Composers and writers know that how you say something is really as important as what you have to say, because after all, being in love or feeling grief are hardly unique experiences, yet they will be forever ripe subjects for poets and composers. How many ways have composers expressed yearning in music? That one emotion alone has been expressed with such extraordinary variety and imagination that one could study the history of music by mapping its course. If the performer of a piece that yearns does not draw on the yearning in her own life, as an actor would, the audience may not feel the yearning that the composer penned into the score.

Writing music is not necessarily about expressing emotions but rather about exploring and discovering feelings and thoughts through the process of working: through improvisation, idea selection, and then putting together (literally *com-posing*) the results into a structure that makes it all comprehensible. Often, one discovers what one "has to say" *through* music rather than bringing already formed nonmusical thoughts to the table, although that is also a completely valid approach. The mechanics and mysteries of music itself—its combinations of tones, timbres, patterns, and pulses—is enough to occupy anyone for a lifetime.

I have heard composition students complain that after studying composing and getting a degree or two, they can't decide what style to write in, what musical world to inhabit. They are not sure what musical vocabulary is honestly their own. This problem is more severe than ever before, as we live in a world where every kind of music from everywhere in the world from every time in history is readily available. It is not that one has nothing to say, but rather that there are too many ways to say it. Studying music needs to be about technique as a way to get at that something we all have to say, and then to find the right means of expression that will allow us to speak, write, and play honestly as ourselves. Increasingly, composers are allowing themselves to combine the conflicting influences that surround them, combining popular and classical musical idioms in personal ways that genuinely reflect their formative experiences with music, forging a new eclecticism that is like fusion cuisine. This is healthy and good for music as an art form.

Composition teachers would do well to challenge the student to know his own mind, to help liberate the imagination, to encourage a student to use those techniques that best allow the student's thoughts to be clearly heard. Emotional clarity is an aspect of technique for composers and performers alike. Even playing scales is an emotional exercise, whether the student is aware of it or not. Scales may be played with a sense of detachment and nobility, with passion, with flair, as if showing off, sullenly, fearfully, and in many other ways, all of which are emotional postures. To enjoy playing a scale is a good technical tactic. What would it really mean to play a scale with absolutely no attitude or emotion?

I once asked students in a theory class at Juilliard to compose a melody that would fit with a given harmonic progression by Brahms. "And you have to love the melody you write," I added. "Oh, no," a student said, "that makes it hard." It certainly raises the bar. It is also likely to make the result significantly better.

The love of music, which originally motivated the student to choose an artistic life, should never be forgotten during training and study. The love of one's art is an aspect of technique. The passion that drives someone to be a musician should be refreshed through imaginative exercises, not dulled by meaningless drills. When that passion is the driving force behind technical discipline, the music will speak, it will say something—and while you may never know what that something is in words, you will know that it is there, and understand it.

ON INTERPRETATION

To interpret a work means to discover and identify with the essence of that work, and to communicate it through faithful execution. A great performer uses technique in the service of the music and does not use the music to display technique. Similarly, the artistic performer does not use a piece to exhibit his own personality but identifies with the spirit and the message of the music. The performer enters into a partnership with the composer, a relationship that is sympathetic and passionate. The depth and variety of the performer's personality is made evident by the extent to which the meaning of the piece is communicated. Through the study and performance of music by Beethoven, for example, a performer discovers and gives voice to feelings within herself that she may not have known were there. Through playing the music of Bach, musicians may experience a profound intellectual, physical, and spiritual awakening that for many is a lifetime journey. This is not merely a matter of interpretation, but of study, contemplation, practice, and service to the art. It is a mistake to think that one performs merely to express oneself. It is much more.

A note-perfect performance that does not realize the essence of the work is of little value. An impassioned performance that is full of inaccuracies is also of little worth.

To be able to connect with the essence of a work, the performer needs to understand himself, to explore his own emotions, and get in touch with his inner life and musical imagination. The artist uses her intelligence and imagination to understand the larger historical and aesthetic context of the work to be performed. Good performers are intuitive people, and the intuitive capability can be strengthened by exercising the imagination.

To divorce the study of technique from the philosophy of interpretation is unartistic. Every technical exercise on an instrument should be played with emotion, as a piece of music. Emotion does not mean passion, necessarily. The calm, poised detachment of an expert archer may be the right emotion for certain exercises. A shift of emotional attitude can suddenly make a hard technical exercise much easier. Engage the imagination even when practicing arpeggios, and the exercise comes alive as music. A good technique serves the imagination and should not be noticed for its own sake.

ON PERFORMING NEW MUSIC

I have never known an actor who would act *only* in Shakespeare, Ibsen, or the works of established modern authors such as

Arthur Miller and Tennessee Williams. Actors want to play new roles, to be the first to create an interpretation, to work with the playwright and participate in the birth of the literature that speaks of her own time and ensures the future of the dramatic art.

However, in the world of classical music there are still many musicians, and audience members too, who lack interest in new music. They use the word *modern* as if it meant "strange" or "dissonant" and behave as if there were only one modern style rather than understand that new music is a world of many cultures and personal voices—endlessly varied, colorful, appealing, challenging, and exciting. (And what's wrong with strange and dissonant, anyway?!)

An actor who has worked in new plays can bring a freshness, spontaneity, and sense of immediacy to classical drama, just as a great classical actor can bring perspective, tradition, pacing, and resonance to modern works. This is true for musicians as well.

What prevents someone from participating in new music? Usually the core of the problem is a lack of imagination. An imaginative performer loves to try new things and is versatile by nature.

An imaginative performer approaches new music with the same care she brings to established repertoire and brings to established repertoire the sense of discovery and vitality learned from new music.

Playing music that no one else has ever played liberates the performer's imagination and challenges him to look within for personal connections to the music that can help bring it alive for the very first time.

Since the second edition of this book, the inclusion of new music on concert programs has become increasingly popular, even with major institutions, and the new generation of classical musicians considers playing new music an important part of their work as artists. The music community has also embraced the work of formerly marginalized composers, including women and people of color. This is not only a significant step forward for inclusion and diversity in the artform, but it will expand the audience for new music and increase its relevance in society as a whole.

HEARING IN SILENCE

To hear in silence means to imagine vividly how music sounds, so vividly that it can be heard in the mind as if it were really being played. To be able to hear music in silence while reading a part or score is an essential skill for a professional musician. Many good musicians can look at printed music and hear it clearly. Some can hear only one line, others entire orchestral scores. Some can hear only what is written for their own instrument, a facility learned by experience but left undeveloped. It could and should be developed, and that is one of the aims of these exercises.

Some composers, especially students, tell me that they are surprised when they first hear their own music played on actual instruments, that it is quite different from what they expected. What did they expect? It is not so odd to be occasionally surprised by an effect made by large orchestral forces, where balance, dynamics, and acoustics play a great role, but certainly in chamber music or in familiar orchestral situations this should not be the case. I believe it means that the composer's ability to hear in silence is not as developed as it should be. Current computer software programs for composition that provide MIDI playback do not help develop the ear, even though they are very helpful in many other ways. By getting an immediate physical playback, the mind's ear is not engaged, and so the ability to imagine music in silence is left out of the process. Far from being rendered irrelevant due to new technology, developing the mind's ear is essential to freeing the imagination. A composer (or any musician) should be able to dream of new musical ideas while reclining on a couch or, even better, on a grassy hillside on a sunny afternoon without a computer or any external device. The brain's the thing.

The key to imagining is memory. A refined memory, capable of hearing in the mind a piece that one has heard previously as if it were happening in the present moment, is the complementary skill to imagining unheard music. By trying to hear loudly in the mind something one has heard before, and then altering the memory slightly, one is already imagining new music. This is a step toward composing.

Try this: remember an event in your life. Tell it out loud with as many details as you can remember. Now tell it again, but change some details or add an unexpected twist. You are, obviously, now telling a story that is fiction. When I have asked children to try this exercise, it is common that for the first part of the exercise, they describe themselves brushing their teeth or eating breakfast and then when asked to change or add something, they typically say a monster crashed through the bathroom mirror or their pet jumped up on the table and ate their breakfast. It is the beginning of storytelling, a step toward writing. To do this exercise with music starts the process of composing in a natural, fun manner. This exercise works with any art form.

Hearing in silence is an important, useful skill for musicians, and it is also a stimulating and worthwhile exercise for anyone wishing to explore her inner life. Silence is increasingly hard to find, but then again you can create it anywhere if you concentrate on the task at hand.

I

EXERCISES TO BE DONE IN SILENCE

Hearing in Your Mind's Ear

> Without a well-developed, mobile imagination, crea-
> tive faculty is by no means possible, not by instinct nor
> intuition nor the aid of external technique.
>
> —KONSTANTIN STANISLAVSKY

ONE DAY AT THE GYM, I noticed a man using an abdominal "crunch" machine in which you bring your legs and arms together by "crunching" your abdominal muscles. This poor guy was pulling down mightily with his arms, and so he was exercising only his arms and probably straining his lower back, without any value to the abdominal muscles he hoped to improve. Then I noticed that all around the gym people were pulling and pushing every which way, in many cases not really doing the exercises they had come to perform. If suddenly the gym were audible as music, it would sound like the halls of a music school in which scales, arpeggios, and technical exercises were being played everywhere sloppily, too fast, and out of tune.

The exercises in this book are subtle, especially in the section in which you are asked to imagine various events and sounds. I tell my students when we do these that no one can tell if they are performing these exercises, well, badly, or at all, for that matter. But they must engage their minds seriously and continually question whether they have done what they set out to do with each exercise.

The Mind's Ear. Bruce Adolphe, Oxford University Press. © Oxford University Press 2021.
DOI: 10.1093/oso/9780197576311.003.0002

Many of the exercises that are described in a sentence or two can take half an hour to accomplish. Sometimes, just getting started is challenging. For example, you are asked in the first exercise to hear in your head the voice of someone you know well reciting a passage from a play or poem. Many people have told me that they find it hard to hear someone's voice reading even one sentence before they lose the sound or it becomes vague. One person said she could hear the voices of famous actors and politicians, but not the voice of a personal acquaintance. But if you make the effort and find that you can suddenly do it, the feeling of making a breakthrough in your creative powers is palpable.

Doing the exercises alone can be an excellent way to broaden your skills, and it can also provide extremely private entertainment on trains, buses, and in waiting rooms. The classroom provides another level for these exercises, however. After a group of students sits in silence together, imagining the sounds and events as read by the teacher, they can share verbal descriptions of their experiences. At one session, it turned out that several people had imagined a string quartet playing Beethoven with a trumpet player as the backstage intruder (see "Imagining a Musically Complicated Situation"). Other similarities and differences provoked very lively and enlightening conversation, and promoted real group spirit.

WARM-UP EXERCISES

Most people find it easier to imagine images than sound. So this is an imagination warm-up that is exclusively visual. The sound version follows.

Warm-up No. 1: Imagining an Image

- Close your eyes.
- Imagine a street, any street.
- In the middle of the street is a chair.
- On the chair is a car.
- On top of the car is a person.
- On the person's head is a musical instrument.
- Balanced on top of the instrument, is a piece of fruit.
- Take a good look at this vision.
- Zoom in. Zoom out.
- Try to see it from different angles.
- Open your eyes.

QUESTIONS

Was the street a real street you know?

Was the chair familiar? Ordinary? From your childhood? Was it a strange chair?

Did you design a new chair in your mind?

Was the car full size? A toy car? A cartoon or drawing of a car?

What color or make of car was it? Did it change?

Was the person someone you know?

Was the person clear or vague in the image? Did (s)he have a face or just a body?

What was this person wearing? Did the person keep changing?

What musical instrument appeared? Did it change? Was it full size or small? Do you play that instrument? Why do you think it was that instrument?

What piece of fruit did you see? Did it change?

MORE QUESTIONS

Did you feel as if you were watching a film or an image that you did not control?

Did the images change by themselves or did you feel yourself making decisions?

Was this hard or easy to do?

If some parts were harder than others, which parts? Why do you think that might have been so?

If you are doing this in a group, how many of you imagined the same instrument or fruit? How many of you imagined a toy car? How many saw a person with no face?

The Point: When you allow your mind to play, you may be surprised. Do not forget that the images you saw are all from your imagination, no matter what the suggestions may be. When you want to do creative work, allow it to happen. Do not be critical; do not interfere. Later on, you can play critic and editor. (See the section called *The Feeling of an Idea: Dreaming and Thinking.*)

Warm-up No. 2: Imagining Sounds

- Close your eyes.
- During the following exercise, listen to the sounds mentioned.
- Whether or not you see the images does not matter.

Imagine the sounds of a busy street.

- Hear the sound of a horse and carriage coming down the street.

- Inside the carriage, a woman is singing a song.
- She is holding a dog, which is barking.
- The horse starts to neigh.
- A motorcycle speeds onto the scene with a blaring radio strapped to the back.
- A man opens a window above the street and screams something.
- Listen to all of this at once.
- Try to focus first on one sound, then another, but keep them all happening.
- Try to hear it from different places on the street.
- Try to hear what the man who opened the window heard inside his apartment.

QUESTIONS

Was this harder, easier, or about the same level of difficulty as Warm Up Exercise No. 1?

If the sound version was more difficult, why do you think that may be?

Is it easier to see images in your mind without sound than it is to hear sounds in your mind without images?

Did you see the scene as well as hear it?

If you did see it, did the visual aspect of the scene seem more or less vivid than the sounds?

What was the woman singing?

Did you recognize the song, or was it something you never heard before?

Were there words?

What kind of voice did she have?

Was she singing loudly or to herself?

What did the man scream?

What kind of voice did he have?

If you saw these people, what did they look like?

Did you see the horse? What did it look like?

How often did the horse neigh?

What was on the radio? Was it clear? Did you recognize it?

Construct your own sound scene and try to hear it. You might begin by imagining variations on the one above.

HEARING VOICES

Choose a short passage from a book, play, poem, or magazine.

- Imagine that you are hearing it being read in the voice of someone you know very well.
- Hear clearly the qualities of the voice: the tone, inflection, vowels and consonants, volume.
- Hear the same voice read the same passage with different emotions.
- Hear the person yell and whisper parts of the passage.
- Choose another person and try the exercise.
- Try to hear yourself reading it as someone else would hear you—do not speak out loud.

RING TONE

Not too long ago, all phones rang with the same sound. Now there are endless ring tones. Some ring tones are tunes or short musical phrases, but others may be animal sounds, sirens, or just about any sound that can get your attention. This exercise is about the ring tones you know, and those you might imagine.

- In your mind hear some of the ring tones that are on your phone. Hear them loudly, as if they were really ringing.
- Next, select some sounds from the real world—a cow mooing, wine glasses clinking, wind chimes, a branching breaking, a wolf howling—and imagine them as ring tones.
- Now select a musical timbre to "sample" in your mind's ear— it could be a musical instrument but it might also be something else, such as a car horn or an elephant's "trumpet."
- Select a short musical phrase from a piece or song you know well.
- Hear that phrase "played" by the timbre you selected.
- For example, you might hear the opening bars of Mozart's *Eine kleine Nachtmusik* trumpeted by an elephant.
- Try this with a variety of sounds and tunes. Do not sing or make any vocal sounds during this exercise and do not use an instrument. Try to hear it all in your mind without external aids.

NOW, ANSWER THE PHONE

Because we spend a lot of time listening to people's disembodied voices speaking to us on a phone right next to our ears or even in our ears (with ear buds), imagining voices and sounds as if they were on a phone is a good way to get the mind's ear in training.

- Now that you have imagined a variety of unusual ring tones, answer the phone (in your imagination, of course.)
- What does the person who has called you say?
- Hear the person speak. Do you recognize the voice?
- Imagine five people whose voices you know well saying the same sentence as if they were speaking to you on your phone.
- Imagine each person's voice with different emotions saying the same thing.
- Now imagine the same people singing that sentence to you.
- Imagine the same people singing, but now without words.
- Turn the person's voice into a musical instrument.
- Listen as the musical instrument becomes another musical instrument.
- Listen as the musical instrument transforms back into the voice of a friend, first without words, and then, finally, speaking words as at the start of this exercise.

THE UNDERSTUDY

- Pick a song or aria you know well; listen carefully to a recording of it; listen more closely than you ever have before.
- Afterward, "play it back" in your memory with total accuracy, paying attention to every detail. Perhaps pretend you are wearing earphones rather than listening on speakers. This may make it more immediate.
- Now, play it back again, but substitute the voice of someone you know for that of the singer on the recording.

VARIATION

Listen to a recording of a concerto.

"Play it back" in your mind, substituting a different instrument for the correct one. (Hear a horn concerto with a clarinet soloist.)

IMAGINING A NEW WORK IN PERFORMANCE

You are in a space (concert hall, church, school) where you love to hear music.

> You are in the audience.
>
> An ensemble of musicians enters; you know them personally.
>
> Picture clearly how they look, what instruments they will play, how they are seated.
>
> They play a work you have never heard before, a work you find thrilling as soon as it begins.
>
> Your program does not list the composer of the work.
>
> Listen to the entire work carefully, following every player. Try to actually hear music in your mind as clearly as if it were really being played.
>
> You are never bored for a moment while this work is performed. Your mind never wanders.
>
> You excitedly leave the performance during intermission and, seeing a friend, describe in words what you loved about the work you have just heard.
>
> Describe the work out loud, trying to articulate accurately what you imagined to be the piece.
>
> Can you really remember passages from the piece? Does it change as you describe it out loud?

IMAGINING A MUSICALLY COMPLICATED SITUATION

Choose an ensemble with which you have some experience: string quartet, wind quintet, brass quintet, etc., as the focus of this exercise.

- You are in the audience at a chamber music concert.
- Picture the performance space in detail.
- The performers (of the ensemble you have chosen) enter. Picture each of them clearly.
- They are playing a piece you know well (select a piece now).
- Hear the piece in detail, loudly (as if it were really happening). Do not be vague.
- Watch the players closely, individually, together.
- Somewhere backstage, someone is practicing.
- The practicing musician can be heard by the ensemble and the audience.
- Although the players continue, you can sense their annoyance—how does this look and sound?
- What instrument is the backstage musician playing?
- What piece is the backstage musician practicing?
- Hear the two pieces (the one onstage and the one backstage) clearly, loudly.

VARIATION

The performers on stage inexplicably and simultaneously begin to play the same music as the backstage musician.

The backstage player abruptly changes pieces, and the on-stage performers go along with the new piece as well.

This keeps happening.

Hear the pieces clearly, loudly in your mind.

Members of the audience begin to sing in four-part harmony.

Hear the ongoing musical chase scene; at the same time hear the audience singing.

You leave the hall alone, everyone else stays and continues singing.

Hear the sounds fade into the distance. Hear the new sounds (street sounds) overtake the musical sounds.

MOZART HAS SOMETHING TO TELL YOU

Try this exercise when you are drowsy and reclining.

- Mozart appears to you in a vision.
- See his face clearly, his clothes, his posture.
- He hovers above you, looks down at you and speaks:
- "I died very young, and had much music left in me to compose. I have chosen you to receive this piece."
- You hear a piece by Mozart that you have never heard (and he never wrote)!
- Hear the opening statement clearly.
- Try to let the piece exist without making it happen.
- Perhaps you sing along with parts of it now and then.

This is a personal favorite of mine, and I do it often. Mozart is a particularly good choice for this exercise because of the profusion of melodic ideas and the elegant balance of predictable and surprising elements in the music. However, if you are not familiar enough with his music, use a composer with whom you are better acquainted for this exercise.

Note: I do not recommend that you try to write this down because that changes the energy of the exercise. Just listen to the piece and enjoy!

HEARING ORDINARY SOUNDS IN YOUR MIND

Part I

Hear the following sounds loudly and clearly in your mind, as if you were listening with earphones to recordings of the actual sounds in reality:

- Breaking Glass
- Siren
- Footsteps coming up marble stairs
- Footsteps walking on mud
- Pencil writing on paper
- Eraser rubbing out some words on paper
- Hammering a nail into a wall

Part II

This exercise adds expressive musical elements to the ordinary sounds above.

- Hear breaking glass in a steady pulsing rhythm with accents every few beats
- Hear a siren, starting very softly in the distance (*pp*); it gets louder as it approaches (crescendo; it is loud and very near (*ff*); it disappears into the distance (diminuendo to silence).
- Hear footsteps rapidly coming up marble stairs in short (staccato) clicks (High heels? Tap shoes?)
- Hear heavy footsteps walking on mud in a slow, ponderous rhythm.
- Hear a pencil writing on paper in very fast, light strokes with sudden silences interrupting every so often.

- Hear an eraser rubbing out some words on paper in long, even strokes followed by sudden rapid short strokes.
- Hear the sound of someone hammering a nail into a wall in a steady, loud rhythm, which then gets faster and lighter.

Part III

This exercise adds structure to the sounds imagined in the exercise above.

Take some of the ordinary sounds with expressive musical elements as described above in "Hearing Ordinary Sounds in Your Mind Part II" and combine them to form a musical work. Make a list on paper, but the actual sounds remain only in your mind. Use only two or three of the sounds at first. The structure is the point, not the number of sounds used.

Here is an example of a possible structure using the sounds from Part II:

Sound of a nail being hammered into a wall in a steady loud rhythm/sound of a siren in the distance getting louder/the nail hammering gets faster and lighter/the siren continues to get louder/hammering gets faster but now louder/the siren is very loud and the hammering is now slow and loud/GLASS BREAKS/ silence/the siren fades away into the distance.

This exercise combines imagining sounds in the mind with fundamental and essential compositional skills. As you can see from the example, it is possible to make a structure from these ordinary sounds, which has a compelling emotional contour. Try making a structure that is funny or creepy using the same sounds. The process of working on the structure will automatically turn up the volume of these sounds in your imagination.

ONE NOTE AND TIMBRE CHANGES

- Hear a single note in your mind.
- Listen to it for at least 5 seconds. (Do not sing, hum, or make any actual sound while imagining the tone.)
- Let the note fade out.
- What instrument was playing the note?
- Hear the same pitch played on a trumpet.
- Now it changes to a muted trumpet.
- It changes to an oboe.
- It changes to a flute, then to clarinet, then to violin.

ONE NOTE AND EXPRESSIVE ARTICULATION CHANGES

- Hear a single note in your mind, played on a violin without vibrato.
- Now the violinist adds vibrato.
- The note begins a crescendo.
- The note is now fortissimo.
- The note now begins a descrescendo.
- Now the note is pianissimo.
- Still pianissimo, the violin now plays a tremolo on the note.
- Hear the note plucked (pizzicato) in a steady beat.
- Now, with the bow (arco), the note is played *sfzp* (a sudden loud, accented articulation which immediately becomes quiet, *piano*.)
- Now the note slides upward in a glissando and fades away into silence.

Even one note can have expressive qualities, and it is good practice for performers to play one note with a variety of expressive goals. It is also a good exercise for composers, conductors, and listeners to imagine varied performances of a single tone.

ONE NOTE TELLS A STORY

This exercise uses the previous two exercises in a new way. Instead of starting by imagining notes with timbres and expressive qualities, begin by thinking of a mood you wish to communicate through music. (Feel free to use one of these moods to get started: scary, silly, joyous, nervous, furious, grief stricken.)

- Imagine a person you know. See the person clearly. Select a mood and imagine a situation where this mood makes sense, and see the person in this situation, in this mood.
- Now turn that little scene into a one-note piece (to be performed only in your mind
- Choose an appropriate musical instrument to play the one note
- Using expressive articulations, dynamics, and rhythms, listen to this piece unfold. (It may be very short, or continue for a minute.)

Here is an example of the musical part this exercise:

- The mood is "furious."
- A trumpet plays a sharply articulated staccato note very loudly.
- After a brief silence, the trumpet explodes in a series of very fast repeated notes (the same one note) interrupted by random silences, no rhythmic pattern discernable, and then suddenly stops.
- This is followed by three loud blasts with silences between them, each longer and louder than the previous one.

VARIATION
Add notes to this exercise, making it more and more musically expressive and interesting. Start by using only two notes, then three notes, etc. This restraint will pay off in that it will feel like a major musical opportunity to imagine/create something new with each new note. Restrictions create a challenge that stimulates the imagination.

SCALES AND TIMBRE CHANGES

- Hear a major scale in your mind.
- Hear it played very slowly on a trumpet.
- Hear it played on a muted trumpet.
- Hear the first four notes on a muted trumpet and the last four notes on an oboe.
- Hear each note of the scale played on a different instrument.

Try This: trumpet, flute, clarinet, French horn, violin, oboe, cello, vibraphone.

VARIATION

There is a good chance you were hearing the scale ascending. Try this exercise now with a descending scale. Try it both ascending and descending using scales other than major.

There is a big difference between reading this exercise and actually doing it. If you can really hear those instrumental colors sounding loudly in your mind, playing the notes of the scale, you are ready for the Hearing Orchestration exercise.

SCALES AND DRONE

- Hear one note, clearly played on an instrument of your choice.
- The same note will now become the tonic of a major scale (C in a C major scale), and it is a drone (or pedal tone).
- Hear a major scale ascending while the tonic note continues to sound. It is as if there were two instruments, one holding the tonic note and the other playing the ascending major scale.
- Listen to the scale ascend slowly, paying attention to each interval formed by the tonic note and each note of the scale. Hear each interval loudly and clearly in your mind before moving on to the next interval.
- When you have reached the octave, imagine the top note as the drone while the scale descends. Again, hear every interval clearly before moving on.

VARIATION
Try this exercise with two timbres instead of one. For example, imagine the drone note played by an unmuted trumpet and the ascending scale by a muted trumpet. Now hear it with the drone played by clarinet and the ascending (or descending) scale played by a violin.

As you imagine these instrumental combinations, allow the "performers" in your mind to be expressive, use vibrato, shade the tones, and shape the line. This will keep the sound vibrant, make the exercise more musical, and also engage more of your imaginative powers, making it easier to stay with the exercise.

HEARING ORCHESTRATION

No.1

This exercise uses only one note.

• Picture an orchestra seated in a rehearsal room or concert hall. See everyone clearly.

Hear the following:

• A trumpet plays a medium-range note, *mf*, and then fades to silence.
A flute plays the same note, *mf*, and then fades to silence.
• The flute continues to play this note and is joined by the trumpet.
• Hear them sounding together; hear the flute louder than the trumpet; hear the trumpet louder than the flute. Now they both fade to silence.
• Hear the same note again, now played in unison by a clarinet and a flute. The flute now fades into silence, leaving the clarinet alone. The clarinet fades into silence.
• The violins now play the same note. They are joined by the clarinet, then the flute, and then the trumpet. Hear them all together. Hear the flute the loudest, then the clarinet the loudest, and finally the violins the loudest. First the flute stops playing, then the clarinet, then the trumpet, leaving only the violins. The violins then fade into silence.

VARIATION
Try this exercise choosing any group of instruments from the orchestra. Use only one note each time you try it. When you feel it is the right moment, add another instrument to the mix,

increase the volume of each instrument or section in turn, and then subtract the instruments, one by one.

It is valuable to attempt this with as many different instrumental combinations as you can. Combine a French horn with an oboe and the cello section. The more combinations you try, the better you will be at imagining the timbres and hearing them clearly in your mind. Repeating the exercise with the same instrumental group is also important.

No. 2

This exercise uses one chord, rather than one note.

- Picture a string orchestra seated in a rehearsal room or concert hall. See everyone clearly.

Hear the following:

- The entire string orchestra—violins, violas, cellos, and basses—plays a unison pitch. The sound is rich and full; the dynamic is piano.
- Now the strings divide into a major chord. Just listen to it.
- Which instruments are playing the root, third, and fifth?
- Are there octave differences? Is it changing (different instruments exchanging notes?)
- The volume of the notes in the chords changes: the tonic is loudest; then the third is loudest; now the fifth is loudest.
- Bring the chord back into balance. Hear it fade into silence.

HAVING MORE FUN WITH THIS
- Start with the major chord again.
- Hear the chord rise slowly in a glissando. Every instrument participates.

- As the chord rises in a glissando there is a diminuendo. The chord seems to be disappearing into the stratosphere.
- Silence.
- Suddenly the entire orchestra plucks (pizzicato) the original chord fortissimo!

VARIATIONS

Try this with a different chord: a minor chord, a dominant seventh, a diminished seventh chord, etc. Try it with an interval instead of a chord, the entire string orchestra playing a major second or a tritone, for example. Try it with a complex, dissonant chord of your choice. (You may decide the notes of the chord in advance, or simply hear a chord played in your mind and then "figure out" what it is by listening carefully to each note.)

No. 3

Picture an orchestra seated in a rehearsal space or concert hall. See everyone.
Hear the following:

- A trumpet plays a medium-range note pianissimo, crescendo to forte, diminuendo to pianissimo.
- The trumpet plays the same note, muted now, mezzo piano and holds it while the basses softly play the same note pizzicato in a steady slow pulse.
- The first violin plays the same pitch very high, tremolo as the trumpet fades away but the basses continue.
- Now, one flute and one clarinet enter together, playing still that same pitch, the flute in a high octave, the clarinet two octaves below.

- Now, the cellos play a trill on the same pitch, and a muted trombone quietly glissandos to and away from the note that the cellos are trilling.

Getting Harder:

- Now, the winds play a minor chord, which has as its root the note that the orchestra has been playing.
- Hear the bassoons on the bottom, the clarinets in the middle, the oboe and flutes on top.
- Switch the oboe and flute notes back and forth.
- Switch the oboe and clarinet notes back and forth.
- The timpanist now plays that one pitch, doubling the pizzicato basses, gradually making a crescendo.
- There is a roll with soft mallets on a suspended cymbal.
- The concertmaster plays a high, dramatic solo while the entire orchestra gradually fades into silence, leaving the violin alone.
- The violin solo ends, and very quietly a harp plays three harmonic tones.

You must try to hear this exercise loudly. Hear real sounds not vague colors. Picture the players, if that helps. Also try the exercise without picturing the players, seeing nothing at all. (Is that dark? Bright? What do you see when you see nothing?)

QUESTION
When you picture the players, do you see distinct people, people you know, or just vague forms with instruments? Do you see faces or blurry images where the faces should be? Can you hear the music clearly while you are seeing vague images of the musicians?

THE CONDUCTOR LEAVES
THE PODIUM

- Imagine you are at an orchestral concert.
- See the concert hall, the musicians, the audience.
- Feel the atmosphere.
- The conductor enters; there is applause.
- The orchestra is playing a piece you know well.
- Hear the music clearly, listening for details. Do not replay a recording of the piece in your mind, but hear a live performance.
- Suddenly, the conductor leaves the podium.

What happens?

> Perhaps the orchestra continues to play as if nothing has happened, but then it gets a bit sloppy and some players stop while others forge ahead; perhaps the audience starts talking while the orchestra plays.
>
> Imagine your own scenario, but hear the music. Hear and see the action vividly.

IN TRAINING

- Imagine you are in a train with other people.
- See each of them clearly; note what they are wearing, their posture, what they are reading or doing, etc.
- Suddenly, one by one, each passenger on the train sings a solo.
- Hear each solo. How does each voice "fit" the singer?
- What do they sing about? Each solo should be short, distinctly different from the other songs, and appropriate to the singer.
- Now they all begin to sing together.
- You arrive at your station and get off the train, hearing the muffled voices behind you as the doors close. Hear the sound of the train drowning out the chorus inside.

VARIATION
This may be acted out by a group, but first, each member of the group should imagine the whole sequence in silence.

A SENSELESS ACTIVITY

- Picture a painting or sculpture you have seen; see it as clearly as you can.
- Recall the smell of a particular food; try to really get the aroma.
- Remember an instrumental piece of music. Really hear it; stay with the piece as long as you can still hear it clearly.

The Point: Could you do the three exercises above equally well? Is your visual memory better than the others? Work on improving your aural memory until it is as good as your visual memory. It is important for a musician to have a vivid aural memory.

PULSE AND ENERGY

Listen to a recording of a fast movement several times, each time with a different sense of what the pulse is. For example, if the piece is in 4/4 time, you may hear the pulse on each quarter of the measure, then on half a measure, then once per measure, then hear a very slow pulse such as once every two measures. Try it with a slow movement, as well.

The number of pulses you feel per phrase has a great psychological effect. This is true in listening as well as in performing. Even a very fast piece can have a peaceful kind of energy if the pulse is heard in large phrases rather than in short cells. Good conductors know this and use it for both practical and interpretive reasons. This is also known in the martial arts, where a series of quick movements is made fluid and simple by thinking of a slow pulse filled with rapid details. Try the exercise with the idea of feeling the energy of the music in different ways.

Use your hands as a conductor would to indicate the various ways you can hear and communicate the pulse, as described above.

By the way, what is *your* tempo? I mean the tempo of your behavior, generally. If you don't think you have one, think about someone else in regard to tempo and perhaps you will understand what I mean. People have inner and outer tempi. The inner tempi relate to our emotions and impulses, and the outer tempi concern speech and movement. Hamlet's inner tempo is presto, but his outer tempo is largo. In trying to imitate someone you know, you instinctively latch onto the subject's tempi. If you don't know your own tempo and how it affects your perceptions, how can you discover the true tempo of a work—not merely the metronome marking, but the weight of the pulse, the interplay of harmonic rhythm and surface dissonance?

Try, as an actor would, to imitate a close acquaintance. It is okay to be irreverent—it goes with the territory. Can you separate how the person moves from how he talks? Is there a tempo that seems to fit his actions or speech? It might make you just a little uncomfortable but ask someone to describe your tempi to you, the speed of your speech and movements. What metronome marking seems to describe your behavior?

READING AND HEARING
PRINTED MUSIC IN SILENCE

Note Exchange

Required: a piece of music manuscript paper, a pencil, any instrument, such as a piano. Do not sing when you do this exercise, as that changes the relationship between your listening and imagining.

> Write a musical phrase consisting of six notes on a piece of music manuscript paper. The notes should be all the same time value, such as six quarter notes or six whole notes. At first, these six notes should be melodically simple—you can make it harder later on.
>
> Play the six notes slowly on the piano (or any instrument) and listen attentively.
>
> Hear the six notes in your mind (in silence).
>
> *Now*: Write the same six notes in a slightly different order, perhaps simply move the first note to the end of the phrase, so that it is now the sixth note.
>
> Hear the newly created phrase in your mind (in silence). Play it on the piano to check yourself.
>
> *Now*: Write the same six notes in yet another order, perhaps a bit more mixed up.
>
> Hear the newly created phrase in your mind (in silence). Play it on the piano to check yourself.
>
> Continue to jumble the notes and then read them, listening to the music in your mind's ear. Always check yourself.

Making It Harder:

> Start with a more challenging melody of six notes, one in
> which the intervals are more difficult for you to hear in
> your mind. You can also make it more difficult by starting
> out with more than six notes.

Note and Rhythm Exchange

Required: A piece of music manuscript paper a pencil, and a
polyphonic instrument, such as a piano, harp, guitar, electric
keyboard, etc. Do not sing when you do this exercise, as that
changes the relationship between your listening and imagining.

> Write a musical phrase consisting of six notes on a piece of
> music manuscript paper. The notes should have a simple
> but distinct rhythm; use sixteenth notes, eighth notes,
> dotted eighth notes, quarter notes, and rests. Keep the
> choice of pitches simple (perhaps diatonic) to begin with.
>
> Play the six-note melody slowly on the piano (or any instru-
> ment) with accurate rhythm and listen attentively.
>
> Hear the notes and the rhythm of the tune in your mind
> (in silence).
>
> *Now:* Keeping the rhythm the same, change the order of the
> pitches in a simple way, perhaps just switching two of
> the notes at first.
>
> Hear the newly created phrase in your mind (in silence)
> with accurate rhythm and pitch. Play it on the piano to
> check yourself.
>
> *Now:* This time, change the order of some of the rhythmic
> units (mix the order of the beats), leaving the notes of
> the tune as they were in the previous version.

Hear the newly created phrase in your mind (in silence). Play it on the piano to check yourself.

Continue to jumble the notes and rhythms in any way you like, notate them clearly, and then read them, listening to the music in your mind's ear. Always check yourself.

Making It Harder: This is easy to make harder! Simply add more pitches and rhythms and keep the mixing process happening.

Chord Exchange

Required: A piece of music manuscript paper, a pencil, any instrument, such as a piano.
Again: Do not sing when you do this exercise, as that changes the relationship between your listening and imagining.

Write out four triads (three-note chords) in root position. The four chords should be of equal time values, such as four whole note chords. At first, just use major and minor. Later, as imagining the sounds in your mind's ear becomes easier, add diminished and augmented triads, and then add seventh chords, ninth chords, etc.

Play the four triads on the piano, listening attentively.

Hear the four chords in your mind (in silence). Check yourself on the piano.

Next: Change the order of the chords, perhaps making the first chord the last. Write this out.

Hear the new chord progression in your mind (in silence). Check yourself on the piano.

Keep reordering the chords, hear them in silence, and then check yourself.

Next: Change the inversions of the chords (write this out, too) and perhaps add a fifth chord.

Continue to imagine the sound of these chord progressions in silence, and then check yourself on the piano.

Hearing a Printed Melody

Required: Printed solo (unaccompanied) music for a single-line melodic instrument (such as the flute or oboe) and a recording of that music or a live performer. Take a page of the sheet music for a solo melodic instrument. In this exercise, you do not create the melody yourself, but use instead a published piece that you do not know.

Listen to one phrase of the music (either live performance or a recording will do) while you read the notes on the page. You may want to listen to the same phrase several times, always keeping your eyes on the printed page.

In silence, read the printed notes and try to play back the music exactly as you heard it.

Now: Try to hear the same music played more slowly. Everything but the tempo remains the same.

Now: Try to hear the music with different articulations or dynamics. Every other aspect of the music should remain the same (pitches, rhythms, timbres.)

This time, after you play back the same phrase in your mind, continue to hear the music that comes next—keep reading the score in silence.

After you have listened in silence to the new phrase (that you have not yet heard performed), play the recording or ask the musician to play. Did you hear the phrase correctly?

Continue through as much of the piece as you can the same way: listen to a phrase; play it back in your mind (in silence); read a new phrase and then listen to that phrase performed. Take your time and repeat this exercise until it comes easily.

The Next Step? Try the same exercise with a two-voice (or two-instrument) piece. Then, move on to a trio or quartet.

DECEPTION IS A GOOD THING
(IN MUSIC, THAT IS)

A fundamental aspect of musical composition is the element of deception or surprise. An unexpected harmony that feels both surprising and yet "right" is a familiar compositional device, used by composers in many styles throughout the history of music. The expression "surprising but inevitable" is often used to describe this practice when it is well done. The element of surprise is common to all dramatic structures, whether in music or in a play, novel, or movie—and there is a unique challenge in the case of instrumental music (without words), where the idea of narrative meaning is necessarily oblique, to discover new, fresh ways to be surprising.

The chord progression V7 to vi (dominant seventh to submediant; in C major: G dominant seventh to A minor) is such a commonly deployed deceptive device—a substitution for the final cadence of V7 to I—that it is actually called the "deceptive cadence" in standard books on theory and music history. By the time this cadence had become so prevalent in music that it earned its nickname, it had become formulaic, a cliché, and ironically it could hardly be considered genuinely deceptive anymore. It is like an old joke that has been told so many times that instead of laughs it elicits only a faint smile or a rolling of the eyes. (And yet when the deceptive cadence is performed sympathetically, with genuine and appropriate emotion, within the context of a musical work, it can still be effective.)

Of course, there are many ways to deceive and so intrigue the listener, and whether the deception is charming or alarming, it always keeps the piece going forward, delaying the inevitable, the final cadence, and so prolonging our enjoyment of the music. Some of the most beautiful moments in music are deceptive resolutions of dissonant harmonies. The way

deceptive resolutions are used by composers is such a significant aspect of musical syntax that it can actually define an individual compositional style or even the common practice of an
entire musical era.

*As a warm up to deceptive musical exercises, the following two
exercises ("Sirens in the Sink" and "Sound Collector") involve creating deceptive situations with everyday sounds. Then we move on
to music.*

Sirens in the Sink

- Imagine yourself in a kitchen where all the appliances and
  fixtures make unexpected sounds.
- You turn on the faucet and it emits a siren sound.
- When the toast is ready, the toaster emits a beautiful bari-
  tone voice singing an aria.
- When you open the refrigerator, it giggles.
- What else do you hear in this kitchen?
- You can turn off each sound after a moment, or you might
  leave it on so that you create a tapestry of sounds, a counterpoint of appliances. Perhaps adjust the volume on each
  (surely the knobs must do that, too) so that you can hear the
  sounds in a good balance.

Sound Collector

*In order to have a surprise, you must first set up expectations. This
exercise uses everyday sounds in a musical context to create a sense of
surprise or deception. Even ordinary sounds can be organized to set up
a listener's expectations, which can then be thwarted—and surprises
can be funny, shocking, disturbing or anything you can dream up.*

- Imagine groups of similar sounds from everyday life. (For example, sounds produced by water might be one group and sounds produced by glass could be another.)
- Hear the sounds you have selected clearly.
- Take time with each sound, letting it take the appropriate amount of time to run its course. (For example, the sound of breaking glass will be relatively brief compared with the sound of rain.)
- Put the sounds in distinct groups. You will need at least two groups to continue the exercise. (For example, Group I could be water—rain, a canoe paddle in a river, water rushing from a faucet, a drip—and Group II could be human sounds such as laughter, coughing, sneezing, and hiccupping.)
- First create a soundscape piece with the sounds of only one group. Hear each sound in the group one at a time, then mix them together, change the order.
- Now, use a sound from a different group to make a deceptive cadence for the first group. (For example: rain on the roof, a dripping faucet, a canoe paddle in a river, then suddenly a cough!)

VARIATIONS

Do the same exercise shown above but with two deceptive cadences, one in the middle and the other at the end.

Another way to add some texture and richness to this exercise is to employ the concept of nonharmonic tones to the deceptive cadence.

Here are some examples you can try:

Suspension: In music, a suspension is a tone held over from a previous chord into a new chord where it is dissonant. Using the exercise above, suspend a sound from Group I into Group II

(For example: the dripping water continues into the coughing sound and then the drips stop.)

Anticipation: In music, an anticipation is a note that anticipates the next harmony.

Using the exercise above, use a single sound from Group II to anticipate (or signal) Group II's arrival. (For example: while the dripping water is sounding, a little bit of coughing appears early and then there is only coughing.)

Dynamic Change: Surprise can come from a sudden dynamic change, especially if it is linked to a harmonic change. Using the exercise above, make a sudden dynamic change right when the Group I ends, as Group II begins. (For example: the dripping water gets louder and louder and suddenly it shifts to very quiet coughing.)

Strange Associations

People with synesthesia involuntarily make extraordinary sensory associations, such as linking colors to musical tones or numbers. One way to free up your imagination is to imagine such connections and to play with the possibilities. Deceptive cadences or surprising resolutions in music are themselves new associations, unexpected but convincing connections. This exercise, therefore, is not only about music but also about smells and colors, opening up your mind to cross-sensory associations. No one but you (and a neuroscientist if you are in an MRI machine) can tell if you are succeeding with this exercise!

- Hear a major chord in your mind, played on three trumpets.
- As you are listening to this chord in your mind's ear, conjure up the smell of almonds.
- Now change the chord to minor and the smell to chocolate.

- Change back to the major chord and the almond aroma.
- Hear any interval of your choice played on a clarinet and a flute.
- As you are listening to this interval, see a color for the clarinet note and a different color for the flute note. Now add an aroma for the clarinet and another aroma for the flute. (Perhaps you are hearing a major ninth, the clarinet's low E is purple and smells like a rose, and the flute's F-sharp is red and smells like a glass of merlot.)
- Hear one note played by a French horn.
- Now imagine that note played very softly and see a dark color.
- Now there is a slow, steady crescendo. As the note gets louder the dark color gets brighter.
- Now the horn plays the same note extremely loudly, and the color is shining bright, almost like metal in the sun. Can you smell something burning?
- Picture a cup of espresso. It emits a tone. What does it sound like?
- Is it low or high? What timbre does it have—is it like a cello, viola, vibraphone, or perhaps a saxophone? Does it have a fast vibrato? Smell the coffee as you listen to its note. Can you taste the espresso?
- Add sugar to the espresso. Smell the sugar. Hear the musical tone sweeten. What happens to the tone? Does the instrument change?

THOUGHT

This exercise has endless possibilities. You can make up many versions of this, mixing music with other senses. But while you can plan out the exercise, as I have above, you can also experiment by surprising yourself. First imagine a musical note, but don't decide in advance what colors or smells will arise—just wait and see what happens.

Scales and Accidentals

• Imagine a major scale being played on a musical instrument you know well.

• Hear the notes clearly, slowly, ascending the scale.

• Now, the scale begins again but one note is wrong. Perhaps that note is louder than all the others.

• Now, the scale begins again but two notes are wrong.

• Try to surprise yourself. Let the wrong note appear without your predicting or manipulating the image. If you do this, you are not only creating a genuinely surprising situation, but you are in the dream state of imagining. You feel as though you are in the audience of your mind's ear. This is an important state for creative thought.

VARIATION NO. 1

Imagine a major scale being played on a clarinet, but one note will be played on an electric guitar. Which note? Surprise yourself. Try this using two other instruments, then with three.

VARIATION NO. 2

Combine the two versions of this exercise shown above: mix the wrong notes with the timbre surprises.

II

EXERCISES INVOLVING GROUPS

No Instruments Needed

THESE EXERCISES CAN BE USED by nonmusicians to develop musical skills, but I have found that music students need and enjoy creative exercises that free them from their instruments now and then. There is a bit of the actor in every talented musician. It is extraordinary that this vital energy is not tapped as a normal part of music training. Musicians should be trained in movement and posture as a matter of course. Alexander Technique has had a great impact on the confidence and health of many musicians, and it is only recently that it has been included in programs for musicians instead of being reserved for actors and dancers.

Theater exercises would be of great use to student conductors, to help them get past merely indicating emotions with artificial facial expressions and body language, to a point where they truly feel them in the moment of performance and so communicate the real thing to the players. Orchestral musicians can tell when a conductor's movements are connected to genuine feelings and they respond by playing with passion themselves. We are lucky to have wonderful examples of such conductors among us now, including Fabio Luisi, Gustavo Dudamel, and Alan Gilbert.

The purpose of this book is neither to relate actual theater games nor to discuss methods actors use to recall and relive emotions, but rather to employ those methods toward

The Mind's Ear. Bruce Adolphe, Oxford University Press. © Oxford University Press 2021.
DOI: 10.1093/oso/9780197576311.003.0003

musical ends. I recommend that those teachers and students who find these group exercises stimulating explore standard theater games further on their own, using the many excellent manuals available, and by inviting actors to visit the classroom.

CONDUCTING A SPEECH

A group memorizes a short speech or poem.

A conductor is selected from the group.

The conductor's task is to shape a performance of the memorized lines by using his hands to indicate tempo, range, color, dynamics, phrasing, pauses, etc.

This involves important skills: quick memorization; group concentration; dramatic (or comic) intuition; conducting skills.

VARIATION

Try an antiphonal performance. Instead of one group, two or more groups are formed, each with its own conductor.

This performance involves the same goals as above, but the conductors must respond to each other as well, trying to shape a contrapuntal reading of the text. This tends to spark more imaginative readings as the concepts of contrast and dialogue emerge. It is also fun and challenging for the members of the group to respond precisely and appropriately to their conductor while listening to the total effect.

CONDUCTING AN IMPROVISATION

> Each person in a group is given a topic on which to impro-
> vise a speech (How to Bake a Cake, Why Blueberries are
> Good for You, The Future of Democracy, Why I Chose to
> Play the Violin, Global Warming, etc.).
>
> The group stands together like a chorus. A conductor cues
> them in and out, directs their dynamics and range,
> shaping their performance rhythmically and emotionally.
>
> Together, they make a piece of contrapuntal choral music,
> which evolves spontaneously and organically. This often
> has very surprising results, sometimes riotously funny,
> sometimes serious and moving.

VARIATION

Instead of everyone making speeches, some members of the
group may make sounds or gestures, or even dance on cue.

HEARING COUNTERPOINT

Three or four people are given sentences to read aloud. The sentences should be interesting in terms of vocabulary and meaning, but not related to each other. (For example: "It is intelligent to know others, but true wisdom is to know one's self." "We say the sun rises and sets, but really it is the earth that is turning," etc.)

The speakers stand in a straight line, each facing a listener at a distance of about four feet. All the speakers say their sentences at the same time, at the same dynamic.

The listeners must concentrate on the speaker opposite them and be able to repeat what was said.

The speakers should repeat their sentences four or five times, always simultaneously.

VARIATION

The listeners may be asked to repeat a sentence of a speaker not directly facing them.

Or they may be told not to look directly at the speaker whose sentence they must learn but rather at another speaker. This might also be tried with eyes closed.

NOISES SIGNIFYING SOMETHING

This is another one borrowed from the drama world.

> A group of people (not more than six) stands in a semicircle behind an individual (the storyteller).
> All of them face the audience (or whoever is not participating at present).
> The members of the group make noises of any kind.
> The storyteller must use these sounds to tell a story, incorporating each sound as soon as she hears it.

MOMENTS OF TRUTH

This exercise is possible only with musicians who can sight-sing fairly well. It is a way of testing a group rather than testing an individual and promotes both good listening skills and a sense of camaraderie.

> A melody with not too wide a range is written on a chalkboard. The first note is played for everyone to hear, and a metronome is set clicking at a comfortable tempo for sight-singing.
>
> Everyone sings the first note, but then continues to hear the music in silence without singing.
>
> At unpredictable moments, the teacher or group leader indicates that they are to sing out loud for a note or two.
>
> Then they return to silent sight-reading until the indication to sing out loud is given again.

Note: This can have shocking results and is an excellent way to develop the mind's ear. It is important to keep a sense of humor about this. There are many reasons that someone might sing the wrong note. The teacher or group leader should correct wrong notes only by playing or singing the correct note without calling attention to who is wrong and who is right. It's a group game that should be fun. It should not be used as a *test*.

III

EXERCISES USING MUSICAL

INSTRUMENTS

THE EXERCISES IN THE NEXT two sections involve playing instruments. While only musicians can actually perform these exercises, it is valuable in a school or master class to have interested nonmusicians attend the class when possible because it provides an unusual opportunity for mingling and sharing, which rehearsals and performances typically do not. Also, the presence of an "audience" is good for the atmosphere during improvisation.

All of these exercises are in fact improvisations of various kinds, yet the focus is not usually on the idea of improvisation itself, but on a specific goal. This is generally the key to good improvising and to freeing the mind for spontaneous action. Asking two students to improvise a duet merely puts them on the spot. Asking them to use their instruments to debate an issue that they are encouraged to imagine in words creates a drama and allows them to engage each other on a moment-to-moment basis.

A slightly different approach is seen in the modal improvisation. Here musical rules are used rather than dramatic suggestion. Rules free rather than bind the imagination. What game has no rules? The rules and boundaries in any game provide the player with challenges and set up the environment for achievement.

The Mind's Ear. Bruce Adolphe, Oxford University Press. © Oxford University Press 2021.
DOI: 10.1093/oso/9780197576311.003.0004

Using these exercises, I have seen students who were truly fearful of improvising transformed into proficient practitioners. The goals and rules not only provide focus, but also promote ensemble spirit, a goal worth achieving even when the improvisation is not wholly successful.

It must be clear to the students that an improvisation should not be listened to as one listens to a composed work. That is one of the values of the Use It! exercise. Use mistakes to spur your imagination rather than shrink from them or stop because of them. A mistake can actually set you free, as many performers know. It happened; it's over, and now you can proceed with that particular fear out of the way! A common metaphor used among performers is that of driving a car: keep your eyes on the road in front of you—*not* on the rearview mirror. (But the rearview mirror concept *can* be useful in *improvisation*, not regarding mistakes but rather in building a structure. See "A Word about Improvisation for Classical Musicians" in the front of this book.)

Some concepts that apply to all the improvisation exercises are: think dramatically, have rules, have goals, enjoy mistakes as well as inspired moments, conclude the improvisation with a real ending emotionally and harmonically.

WHO IS LISTENING?

This exercise is for performers, both instrumentalists and singers.

In discussions and interviews with performing artists, I have discovered that performers' attitudes toward audiences vary enormously.

Some musicians have told me that they notice the audience only before and after they play, that while they are playing they enter the music only and shut the audience out of their minds. Other musicians have said that relating to the audience is essential while playing and that an attentive, interested audience raises their level of performance.

Most musicians I know feel that recording in a studio or in an empty concert hall has its good and bad aspects: the lack of audience makes the performer feel less energized than at a concert because the desire to communicate, to reach out to the listeners must be imagined, perhaps by thinking of the people who will listen to the recording once it is released. Yet without an audience there is also a kind of freedom to explore more intimate emotions that may not reach past the first few rows of a concert hall, and there is less pressure since it is possible to record things over.

During the 2020 pandemic, musicians around the world were suddenly unable to perform for live audiences as concerts everywhere were canceled and concert halls closed their doors. Many musicians, for the first time in their lives, performed in their homes and recorded or streamed concerts using smartphones, computers, iPads, or video cameras. The question of how a live audience—or the lack of one—affects a performer's emotions and energy truly hit home. Performers experienced a strange new mix of distance and intimacy.

Imagining an audience, as some musicians do in a recording studio, is a good exercise. Who is listening? What kind of listener do you want? How might the imagined audience affect the way you play?

Choose a piece you know, love, and can play from memory. Play it imagining the following audiences:

- Everyone listening is a member of your family.
- The entire audience is staying at an inn together (perhaps for the week prior to the concert), having meals together in a large dining room, and going on walks together every afternoon. You are also staying at the inn. Many of the audience members are artists whose work you know, writers whose books you have read, and actors whose performances or movies you have seen. You respect them and know them. It is your turn to share some of your artistry.
- The audience is a group of patients in a hospital ward. (Why are they there? What do they have in common?) Your musical performance could be an essential part of their healing.
- The audience is made up of soldiers who are soon being sent into battle.
- The audience is made of people who have never heard or seen the instrument you are playing, and it is your job to convince them it is a worthwhile musical device for performing.
- The audience is a visiting group from another planet who has never seen or heard any music from the planet Earth.

PERFORM AS IF FOR ONE
LISTENER ONLY

In the previous exercise ("Who Is Listening?"), you imagined audiences of different types. Another way to use your imagination during performance is to pick one person from the audience and play for that person only.

This exercise may be practiced at home or in a studio, but the more significant use of this exercise is in an actual concert situation. If you are playing a beautiful, lyrical, romantic *adagio* or a soul-searching nocturne, this exercise may help bring genuine intimacy to the music.

Your audience may be large—perhaps hundreds of people—but you are going to play to one person only. The person should be your favorite person to play for—your spouse or significant other, a close relative, or anyone with whom you can open up, be yourself, and not feel judged while performing. Picture that person in the audience in a particular seat. (The person need not actually be in the audience.) The rest of the audience is in darkness; perhaps they even disappear. A spotlight illuminates your chosen listener. Now play!

IF STANISLAVSKI WERE YOUR VIOLIN TEACHER

If Konstantin Stanislavski—the great actor, director, and teacher of acting—were your violin teacher, your lesson might go something like this:

Play "The Star-Spangled Banner."

> How would you play it if you had been in a concentration camp that was just liberated by the American troops? Play it that way.
>
> How would you play it if you were a hostage in a U.S. Embassy, and the terrorists said that you would all be freed if your rendition of "The Star-Spangled Banner" pleased them? Play it that way.
>
> How would you play it if you were protesting U.S. foreign policy by performing "The Star-Spangled Banner" on the steps of the White House while someone burned a flag? Play it that way.
>
> How would you play it if you were on your honeymoon and your new spouse asked you to play it romantically after dinner?

Of course, you may use any instrument for this exercise, including voice (which makes it even more like an acting exercise.)

This exercise asks many questions of the performer by requiring her to imagine very emotionally charged situations as background to the performance.

> How does your own emotional state affect your performance?
>
> If you substituted a work of great artistic integrity in place of "The Star-Spangled Banner," would your performance change in the same way?

How do you enter the emotional world of a piece of music when you feel distracted or upset by external circumstances?

Do you—should you—use your irrelevant emotional state by letting the energy fuel and possibly alter your interpretation, or should you let the piece draw you back from your "real life" into the musical life of the composer and the specific work you are to perform?

How clearly defined is your sense of the emotional and dramatic energy of the piece? How carefully have you examined its emotional tone, pacing, structure, and range?

How does your inner life connect with the spirit of the time in which the work was conceived?

What are your feelings about "authentic" performance practice? Are your feelings authentic?

All of these questions and many others need to be asked over and over. In real life, a musician is not an actor and should not pretend to be another person—not even the composer—during a concert performance. However, doing so as an exercise may help liberate you from performance anxieties and free you of some habits. And yet, probing the imagination with questions about one's inner life with respect to performance is vital and basic for musicians who hope to realize the emotional truth of a great work.

Imagining circumstances like those in the exercises above may seem extreme, but all circumstances affect behavior—the practice room and master class no less than the concert hall or recording studio—and the technique of imagining can be very useful on a simply practical level as well as a means to general emotional awareness.

Further suggestions for the Stanislavski exercise:

> This time, instead of a song like "The Star-Spangled Banner," choose a great piece of music and imagine playing it in an inappropriate situation.
>
> How would you play a slow movement of a Beethoven sonata if you were the third act in a vaudeville show?
>
> How would you play it if the audience were a room full of restless five-year-old children who were expecting you to entertain them (you may not change the piece!).

If you allow yourself to try exercises that make you uncomfortable—such as playing a serious philosophical movement at a vaudeville show—you may discover aspects of the piece and of yourself of which you were unaware.

Hearing music with unfamiliar ears (the ears of your imagined listeners who are so unlike you) can be a revelation. As a technique, hearing yourself perform as if you were a different type of listener than you actually are is a way to further explore and understand how you do listen.

PLAY THE MOONLIGHT SONATA
FOR LAUGHS

This exercise is fully described in the title.

Play the first movement of Beethoven's *Moonlight Sonata* (or a similarly serious, beautiful piece) irreverently for comic effect.

An actor might get to know a text by playing with it in every conceivable way. No actor would find it dishonorable, in a rehearsal or as an exercise, to make a comedy out of a great Shakespearian soliloquy. For some reason, many musicians do not share this playfulness with regard to great works. But if you revere or worship a work as if it were a holy relic, you will not be able to get your hands on it or sink your teeth into it. A great work will survive your experiments. In fact, you will love it all the more when you can see it without the halo you have placed above it. Get to know it as if it were a member of your family whom you would tease, argue with, and love.

SOLILOQUY BY SHAKESPEARE
SANS WORDS

A solo musician (on any instrument) places on a music stand a famous soliloquy by Shakespeare and proceeds to "speak" it on the instrument. The player should use the rhythm and inflection of speech to guide the performance. No words are spoken; the text becomes the subtext. The musical recitation must be syllabic in order for the idea to be productive.

It can be extremely effective on the piano, and I suggest that even nonpianists can do this at the keyboard. There are many levels at which this can work. At the fundamental level, the inflection of the speech is the only guide to the performance, and the player should not worry about musical style or even what notes to play. At this level, only inflection, range, dynamics, and tempo are to be considered.

At a more advanced level, the performer may pick a musical model that will influence the outcome of the improvisation. Some useful models are the recitatives of the Evangelist in Bach's *St. John Passion*, the *sprechgesang* approach in Schoenberg's *Pierrot lunaire*; recitative in Mozart's operas, Berg's operas *Wozzeck* and *Lulu*. Obviously, the list could go on. Using a musical model as a guide to the improvisational style makes the exercise more challenging and helps to focus the student's imagination.

If there is a class (rather than a private lesson), then it is very helpful to give all the students copies of the speeches to be used for the improvisation. It is important to give feedback concerning the quality of the improvisation. It is also advisable to stop the student in mid-phrase if the mood is lost or if the class cannot follow the speech because the performer's recitation is vague or meandering, or if the rhythmic articulations of the music do not match the syllables in the speech, leading to confusion. I recommend that the students try reading the lines out loud first, then proceed to the instrumental improvisation.

NO EXIT

Playing slow movements can be more difficult than playing fast ones, not only in terms of tone quality but also emotionally and architecturally. Allowing the music to speak fully, not rushing, finding the expansiveness necessary is a challenge.

> Imagine that you have been told by the authorities (in some totalitarian situation, perhaps) that you may play one piece of music, but it will be your last. When it is over, they will arrest you, and send you to prison for a long time.
>
> You must play this piece slowly, make it last, delay the ending, spend time on every gesture, get the most out of it. You don't want it to ever end, do you?

When trying this exercise, it is best to play the same slow movement first without imagining this scenario. Then try the exercise. If there is a class listening to these two renditions, students should not be informed of the scenario (or subtext). Then, they should compare the two performances.

PIANO IS MY FORTE

In Baroque performance practice, there are many approaches to playing dynamics that are not notated. Terraced dynamics, or the echo effect, is one example. But in later music, composers treated dynamics quite differently, and it became necessary to notate them or performers would not play the music as the composer intended.

Beethoven's music is full of sudden dynamic changes that may be shocking, comic, or dramatic. They are probably the result of his improvisations, where he felt the audience's mood and so changed course suddenly, enjoying that he could control the reactions of the aristocracy with a mere sforzando or sudden fortissimo. We would not know that we should play these dynamic changes if Beethoven had not notated them. Or would we? Can the music itself *suggest* dynamics?

The idea of this exercise is to experiment with dynamics when the original markings have been removed from the score.

> Using white-out on a photocopy or some other simple means, remove all the dynamic markings from a piece by Beethoven.
>
> The player then reads from this score, playing dynamics in any way that seems to fit the music.
>
> How many different dynamic versions can you play and still make the music convincing? Did any of your versions happen to match what Beethoven actually wrote?

YOU ARE GLENN GOULD

This is for instrumentalists.

Imagine a famous performer whose playing you know well.

Play a piece you know as if you were that person.

Do not imitate! Be that person.

Think, feel, and play as that person. For example, play a movement of a Beethoven piano sonata as if you were Rudolf Serkin, Artur Rubinstein, Glenn Gould, Martha Argerich, Maurizio Pollini, or Richard Goode.

Play a Bach violin partita as if you were Gidon Kremer, Henryk Szerying, Itzhak Perlman, Midori, Joshua Bell, Daniel Hope, or Jaap Schroeder.

This may seem to be difficult but it is a rewarding exercise.

- Can you clearly define the differences among these players?
- Can you hear these qualities in your mind?
- Can you sound like these players by imagining yourself to be them?
- Does analyzing their playing help you to focus on the specific qualities or does that make it more difficult?
- Is this about technique or feeling? How are they separate ideas?
- Does it help to go for details or the big picture?

PLAYING IN THE DARK

One of Chopin's students asked him why he stared into space when he played. Chopin answered that this is a result of his practicing in the dark. Chopin advised his students to practice in the dark in order to sharpen their listening skills, to allow them to focus exclusively on sound, tone, clarity, exact pedaling, articulation, and dynamics.

Take Chopin's advice. There are several ways to do this:

Memorize a piece of music, or part of a piece. Then practice it in the dark, being very attentive to every aspect of the sound.

For pianists: Play a simple chord progression in the dark. Listen for balance among the voices, for weight and resonance. Play the chords at different tempi, with different dynamics and articulation.

Play a phrase as softly as you can, letting it float in the darkness. How clear is your tone? How clean is the articulation? How does the first note break the silence? How does the last note lead back into silence?

Improvise in the dark. You might even pretend someone else is playing and you are the listener. This can free up your imagination.

TEMPO CHANGE-O

If you give a musician a Baroque dance movement to play—an allemande, sarabande, gavotte, or gigue—it is clear what a good tempo might be, even if the name of the dance or tempo marking is not printed on the page. This is because the characteristics of the music are familiar, traditions are well known, and the rhythms clearly define the dance. But finding a good tempo is not always easy. Even with dance movements, especially those by Bach for unaccompanied string instruments, there is much disagreement among performers when it comes to tempi. With many pieces of music, we take the composer's tempo indication (or a metronome mark) as the obvious guide, but what if there were no such guidance at the top of the printed music?

If there is a group of students and a teacher, a good approach to exploring tempo is this:

> The teacher *removes* (or covers) the tempo indications from a piece of unfamiliar music and asks students to figure out a good tempo by playing the piece at different speeds. When is it convincing? At which tempo does the music seem to work best? Why?

This can also work with music one already knows:

- Play a fast movement very slowly, and try to make it compelling.
- Play a slow movement quickly. Can you make it work?

PLAYING CRITIC

- Choose a piece you know well.
- Ideally, it should be a piece you can play from memory.
- Think of the words a critic might use to describe a great performance of this particular work.
- Play the piece that way.
- Think of words a critic might use to describe a poor performance of this work.
- Play the piece that way.

Note: When Itzhak Perlman was reading through a new work I had composed for him, he noticed that I had not put a descriptive term at the top of the piece along with the tempo marking. He suggested I write "Play Fantastically"!

HELLO, HOW ARE YOU?

An actor can say a simple sentence such as "Hello, how are you?" so that it communicates a variety of subtexts.

Try to say "Hello, how are you?" as if:

- Addressing a long-lost friend.
- Bumping into someone you were trying to avoid.
- Meeting someone you have admired all your life and never expected to meet.
- Addressing someone you suspect detests you.
- Addressing someone you find attractive.
- Greeting someone who is about to interview you for an important job.

This list could go on and on. Make up your own situations and try it again. Next, make up a different short sentence or a longer, more complicated sentence and try the exercise again.

Musical phrases cannot be performed with as much variation as spoken text can; unlike in speech, the pitch and rhythm are given. However, there is a wide range of possible interpretations of a phrase, as any two performances will prove.

How many different deliveries can you give a phrase and still be true to what is written?

Pick a musical phrase which is long enough to be usable for this exercise—even a complete theme may be used—and play it as many ways as you can think of without distorting its rhythm or dynamics.

BE A FICTIONAL PERSON

This exercise is for performers. It is not terribly unusual for a young violinist to pretend to be a famous performer such as Itzhak Perlman or Midori in order to play with new energy and feel liberated from habits, but here is an exercise that offers a strange twist on that idea...perhaps an Oliver Twist.

Choose a character from a novel or play. It should be someone whose personality you have thought about and who perhaps you might want to be cast as in a movie version of the story.

Now that you have chosen the character, select a location or setting from the novel or play and a background situation. Where is your character at this moment? What is going on at this point in the story? What is your character feeling? What is on his or her mind?

It so happens (in this exercise) that the character plays a musical instrument (the same one you play.) You are about to add a scene to the story. It is important that you must remain in character throughout the exercise.

Take your instrument out of its case (if possible) as that character would. Think of the time period, the scene, the mood. Imagine you are being filmed.

Play a scale as that fictional character at that moment and in that place you have chosen from the story. Before you play another scale, do something that character might do (look in the mirror, weep, stare into space, chuckle inwardly, make a phone call, eat cake...). Now play another scale, still in character.

Play a movement of a piece as that character.

Now, another character or perhaps several characters from the novel (or play) come into the room to listen to your character play the piece.

Play it for them, keeping in mind the background drama, the place, and the relationship(s) involved.

Now pick another character from the same story and try this exercise again. Next, choose another novel or play that is as different from the first one as possible, and try it again.

USE IT!

This exercise requires a pianist and an "annoying bystander."

The pianist improvises a short phrase that should have a clear harmonic progression, must be tonal, and have a simple, memorable rhythmic outline. At the completion of the phrase, the bystander plays any one note on the piano. The pianist then must use that note as the first note in the next phrase, making it sound like it was the note that should have been played.

To make this amusing and effective, the bystander should purposely play notes that are not part of the progression just heard. For example, if the pianist plays a phrase in C major ending on the dominant, the bystander might play a C sharp. The pianist then modulates gracefully to D minor using the rhythm of his original phrase to give the illusion that this was the next phrase of the "piece" he was going to play. Of course, that is not the only solution to the unexpected C sharp. The pianist could use that C sharp as an appoggiatura and then keep the appoggiatura going as a *motif*. The pianist might use the C sharp as a D flat (who knew it was a C sharp anyway?) and go via the Neapolitan to C minor, or play the German augmented sixth chord of F major and get right back to C major.

Obviously, the performer's fluency in harmony matters more in this exercise than in most of the others presented here. However, it is the pianist's *ear for harmony* and his practical keyboard skills that are called into play, not necessarily his *theoretical* knowledge (though it can help). I have frequently observed that a performer's "ear" and skill are not necessarily the same as his "knowledge." (Also, sometimes a student's theoretical knowledge is not put to practical use at the keyboard, and this exercise can help put them in alignment.)

ACCOMPANIED POETRY READING

Two people are needed: a reader and an instrumentalist.

The reader recites a poem while the instrumentalist improvises a musical setting. There should be no rehearsal and no discussion before they begin.

The reader starts and the player begins a moment later.

The mood, rhythm and energy of the poem, as well as the phrase lengths, are the musician's cues.

Of course, the reader may react to the music, as well, and so the performance will be interactive. It is important to pick different types of poetry with which to experiment in order to get the full impact of this exercise. Try Japanese Haiku, poetry by Edgar Allan Poe, William Carlos Williams, Jerome Rothenberg, Billy Collins, Rita Dove, etc.

As with many of these exercises, the performers' seriousness of intent is vital to the success of their collaboration. It is amazing what can happen when spontaneity, freedom, and performance energy are focused on a given task before a supportive audience.

VARIATIONS

Give the performance an imaginary setting to see if that affects the style of the performers: a café, Carnegie Hall, a barn, a county fair, a hospital, a campground, a dark forest, the moon. The reader could memorize the poem and then the performance might take place in the dark (lights out).

AN INTRIGUING PERFORMANCE (OR THE SPY GAME)

Play a few phrases from a piece of music or perhaps an entire movement.

Now, play the same phrases or movement but imagine while you are playing that the music contains a secret message in code that one member of the audience is waiting to hear.

When she hears and understands the message, she will leave the auditorium and make an important phone call. You don't know what the message is, but you do know that your playing is the vehicle by which the message is to be delivered.

You might imagine that you are a spy whose "cover" is that of a musician, and the secret message is of grave importance.

Has this changed the way you play the music? How?

In my experience with this exercise, performers want to project the secret message, and so they become more focused on clarity of detail, precise rhythmic inflection, and clear, natural phrasing. They feel that communicating the message encoded in the music is of uppermost importance and so they do not display their own egos while playing.

Is there a message in music that needs to be communicated?
Is there something "encoded" in the notes, rhythms, inflections, and dynamics?
Can you be sure what that message is?
Can someone else understand the music in a different way than the performer understands it?

Isn't it a good feeling to play to an understanding, fully engaged audience member?

In pretending to be a spy who must musically send out a message in code, some performers get closer to the music's essence, and project the music with a sense of mission that improves the performance. Shouldn't a performer's goal always be to project the essence of the music?

THE PHRASE-BY-PHRASE
IMPROVISATION FOR TWO

This exercise may be performed with two players at the piano or with any two instruments.

> **Player 1** improvises a short phrase that clearly establishes a mood, idiom, and tempo.
>
> **Player 2** plays the next phase, which must both respond to and extend the first phrase.
>
> **Players 1 & 2** continue to alternate in this manner for as long as they can keep it interesting. It should have a real ending when the time comes, not merely stop.

Are two minds better than one? (I'm of two minds about the answer to that question.)

VARIATION

Give the improvisation a musical problem or conflict to be "enacted" by the players. For example, perhaps the first player improvises in the Dorian mode and the second player improvises in D major. There is a conflict! The resolution to be achieved during the improvisation is for one player to convince the other to change modes, or perhaps for both players to use both Dorian and D major, switching back and forth and mixing them together.

With this method of back-and-forth musical dialogue, there will be surprises for both performers. Surprises spur the imagination and will improve the improvisational skill of both participants.

THE DEBATE FOR TWO PLAYERS

For this exercise, two musicians with instruments are needed.

Player 1 thinks of a sentence to say to Player 2, but instead of saying it with words, plays it on the instrument. This is significantly different from the previous exercise, because here the players are imagining *spoken dialogue* as they play.

Player 2 listens to this "sentence" and responds as if in a debate: the other player's idea must be considered but responded to with an opposing idea.

Players 1 & 2 continue this debate, each trying to convince the other player of the worth of his own point of view while refuting the other's.

After trying this exercise, take a look at a piece of music together to see if there is any "debating" in the music. Think of it this way: After the first phrase or idea in a piece of music, the second phrase might seem to agree, affirm, answer, oppose, or ignore the first phrase. Look at some music with this in mind. In what other ways can two phrases be related?

MIRROR GAME

This requires two players.

One performer (leader) starts by improvising a short phrase. The other performer (mirror player) follows by playing a mirror version of the "same" phrase of music (freely, no need to be exact in terms of intervals). For this game, "mirror version" means to play in the *opposite direction* and the opposite *dynamics* and *articulation* of the leader's phrases. What went up, goes down; what got louder, gets softer; what got faster, gets slower; what was staccato, is legato, etc.

Ideally, the mirror player should play in the style of the leader, so it may be helpful if the two players in this game are able to improvise in the same genre. However, if might also be a fun and instructive version of the game for the mirror player to play in a different style from the leader.

Note: The leader's phrases should at first be brief, but eventually they may increase in length. The leader might get an idea from the mirror player's improvisation. Since the leader does not have to *react* to the mirror player's music, the leader might instead *continue* what the mirror player improvised (which was a mirror-response to the leader to begin with).

KEYBOARD CLUSTERS

For pianists or non-pianists who are willing to play the piano for this cluster-filled exercise!

This exercise frees the pianist to improvise *shapes* and *structures* without having to play any particular notes for melodies and harmonies. All notes are right notes! The player may play single notes, chords, clusters, anything at all during this improvised solo. What matters is shape and form. It might be a rondo, sonata, pop song, a recitative, a dance, or any other form.

It would make the improvisation more fun and instructive for the listeners if the *form* or *idea* of the improvised "piece" is stated before playing. That way, the audience (class) can follow the performer's thought process, and afterward the audience might give feedback. Could they follow the structure? What was most effective in this clustery improvisation? The problem of note-choice is gone, so go all out for the dramatic shape, dynamics, articulations, rhythms, and surprises!

This exercise is inspired by the use of gibberish in theater games, particularly those created by Viola Spolin, a major figure in the development of improvisational theater games in America.

MOODY WORD GAME

Everyone in the group should write one mood-word on a small piece of paper. The words should be good for inspiring musical improvisation, such as: joyous, gloomy, scared, angry, etc.

All the pieces of paper (one word on each) are put into a hat. Someone mixes the papers around and then pulls out one word.

A solo musician or a small ensemble of musicians is selected from the group.

The word is whispered secretly to the selected musician(s). The soloist or group then has a brief secret huddle to decide how they are going to "play" this word to the rest of the group.

The word is performed as a musical improvisation.

The rest of the group guesses what word was performed during the improvisation.

If the group gets the word, or a close-enough word, a new word is selected, and the game continues. The same players may try the new word or give others a chance to try.

If the word is not guessed, and no word that is guessed is at all close to the secret word, then there should be a discussion about what the music sounded like to the group to try to clarify the problem of communication. The teacher or leader might at this point speak privately to the improvisers, suggesting some ideas to improve their performance in terms of communicating the word better.

Next, review the words chosen and the improvisations based on those words to discover what in the music communicated the word or idea successfully and what did not work. When discussing the improvisations and the words, be specific. For example, you might say something like: "Since the word was 'gloomy,' it made sense to play minor harmonies, low notes, and dense textures. It did not help to play fast dramatic music because it changed the mood from gloomy to scary. The dissonances were appropriate at first, but then they became too tense and the mood changed from gloomy to desperate and angry, especially when the rhythms became agitated."

Another interesting aspect of this exercise is the listener's role. When a listener is trying to understand the music—to guess a word, in this case—the listener's role is active and engaged. The listener tends to pay more attention to the music itself rather than to the performer's skill. The listener is aware that the music "means" something and is trying to discover what that meaning could be. This may make the listener less judgmental and more open to the moment. How do you *usually* listen to music?

MODAL IMPROVISATION FOR THREE

This is a good way to get improvisational skills going. Every musician should try improvising, but some feel inhibited or self-conscious. By giving musical and dramatic guidelines, an instructor can free up a hesitant participant.

Choose three instruments (perhaps two treble and one bass, such as flute, violin, and cello—but any combination can work).

All three will improvise in the Dorian mode (D to D).

No sharps or flats allowed.

All phrases must begin and end on either D or A.

One player plays an ostinato or groove (they must make one up) in a regular rhythm with a clear pulse.

After that is established, a second player plays long tones, playing off the ostinato rhythmically, sometimes on the beat, sometimes syncopated, perhaps using effects such as trills or harmonics to create atmosphere.

After that is established, a third player adds much faster music, consisting of scale passages (always Dorian) that move up and down in syncopated, jazzy rhythms. This player should be careful not to play continually, but to rest now and then, allowing the music to breathe.

With a signal from the teacher or another student, the members of the ensemble switch roles in a predetermined manner, trying to continue the music that has been improvised up to that point.

VARIATIONS

If this works well, try adding new elements on a signal from the teacher or a member of the ensemble. New elements might be: one chromatic note (a C sharp?), a technique such as pizzicato or tremolo, sforzando, repeated tones.

ANOTHER VARIATION

Structure the improvisation. Articulation, dynamics, and tempo can be used to define the structure. For example, the music could be divided into three sections, each with its own tempo and some distinct characteristics, such as pianissimo, pizzicato, or legato.

Perhaps the first section is Andante and is performed pianissimo and pizzicato. The second section might be Allegro and is performed forte and arco. What should the third section be?

One More Idea: A conductor may cue the musicians as to dynamics and tempo, helping shape the improvisation.

RHYTHM FIRST

Part I: A Group Improvisation

Rhythm drives improvisation. Rhythmic communication among members of an ensemble is essential and a new group of improvisers would do well to explore rhythm together first, before bringing melody and harmony into the mix. This exercise may be done with drums of any kind, on tabletops or desks, or with any drum substitute on which rhythms can be played with the hands and shared among a group.

For this exercise, at least three people should participate in a group. I will use four imaginary group members to describe the procedure, which may be easily adjusted for different size ensembles.

- Let's call the four members of this group A, B, C, and D.
- A makes up a short, catchy rhythm and plays it.
- Everyone plays A's rhythm together in unison.
- Then B makes up a rhythm and plays it.
- Everyone plays B's rhythm together in unison.
- Now everyone plays both A's rhythm and B's rhythm together in unison.
- C makes up a rhythm and plays it.
- Everyone plays C's rhythm together in unison.
- D makes up a rhythm.
- Everyone plays D's rhythm together in unison.
- Now everyone plays the rhythms of A, B, C, and D together in unison.

Part II

This is a continuation of Part I and is significantly more challenging. Part I should be played easily and with variety before moving on to Part II.

In this exercise, the group may use the rhythms from Part I or make up new ones. As in Part I, each member of the group should create a rhythm and everyone should play it back in unison. Before beginning the exercise, the rhythm patterns should be agreed upon.

> The group plays all the brief rhythmic patterns in a row, then, without stopping, plays them in reverse order. Do this several times. Perhaps play each rhythm three times before moving on to the next, and then play each rhythm three times in reverse order.
>
> Now, play all the rhythms in a new tempo (significantly faster or slower) that is determined and communicated by a group leader only by drumming. Each member of the group should be a leader in turn, each creating a new tempo.
>
> Next, each group member plays a solo that is completely free—it may or may not make use of the rhythms the group has been playing.
>
> In between each solo, the group plays all four of the previous rhythms in forward and backward order, always in a new tempo determined by a leader. Once this gets going, it can be very exciting and involving for all the players and for listeners. The forward and backward drumming in different tempi interspersed by solos is a good structure for improvisation.
>
> Leaders can start to add in dynamics, suddenly playing a rhythm very quietly and the next rhythm loudly.

As the group warms up and everyone "locks in" to the leader's cues and feels the group energy, a new level of improvisational skill will be achieved, as well as skills that relate to performance in any kind of ensemble.

Feel free to take the basic idea of this exercise—solo improvisations, group imitation, changes in tempo, etc.—and use it in any way that fits the group of people involved. However, it is important that the group follow a set of guidelines to the improvisation from start to finish. This enhances listening skills, improvisational ability, and ensemble cooperation.

Part III: Adding Melody

Part II should be played fluently several times and with rhythmic variety before moving on to Part III. This rather difficult exercise is only possible for musicians who play melodic instruments (strings, winds, brass, pitched percussion, etc.) It may be done with voice, and if so, it is advisable not to use words, but rather to "scat" spontaneously.

It is a good idea to add only one melodic instrument to the drumming group to begin with, and then gradually replace most or all of the drums with melodic instruments, depending on circumstances. The easiest way to achieve this is to start with an ensemble that already plays together regularly, such as a wind quintet or brass quintet. You start with all five musicians playing drums (or tabletops). Next, you will have four drummers and a flutist (for example.) Eventually, your ensemble will return to its original formation as a wind quintet, etc. It can be very useful for a student ensemble of any kind to play drums together, doing these exercises to hone their communication skills.

The melodic instrument player will play only in the Dorian mode starting on the note D (D up to the octave higher

D, no sharps or flats. The Dorian mode is excellent for improvisation.) All cadences should end with either the note D or A.

The final cadence for the improvisation should end on the note D.

The improvisation is still based on rhythm.

The rhythmic structure is the same as in Part II, but now melodic music based on the Dorian mode is added into the mix.

Establish four rhythms (or more), play them in order and backwards in unison.

A leader determines the various tempos, as before.

The flutist (or violinist, etc.) plays the rhythmic patterns along with the group.

As before, each player takes a solo, and the melodic player is completely free within the Dorian mode to play any kind of rhythm, dynamic, articulation, range, and expressive feeling. The player should signal clearly when the solo is over.

In between each solo, the group plays all four rhythms in forward and backward order, always in a new tempo determined by a leader.

Next, instead of solos, the musicians play duets. Perhaps a drummer plays with a flutist or perhaps a violinist and clarinetist perform an improvised duet in the Dorian mode. During the duets, the two players should play in the same tempo, energy, and mood. To make this easier to accomplish, one of the two players may be chosen to lead the duet. After a while, instead of a leader and follower, the two players might have a spontaneous dialogue. Again, one of the players should signal the group that the solo is over.

The improvisation ends with all four rhythms played forward and backward.

Feel free to add new ideas and elements to this improvisation or to take off in a completely new direction. Perhaps there are solos alternating with duets. Perhaps each solo is in a new and contrasting mood. Have fun, always be expressive, enjoy mishaps and collisions with humor rather than stop and criticize them. Keep going if possible. Strive for structural clarity and group energy.

TELL ME SOMETHING—ANYTHING!

In an interview, the actor Richard Burton described what it felt like to perform the role of Hamlet night after night for a long run, always striving to be fresh and spontaneous, not wanting the role to get stale after many performances. Feeling numb from so many repetitions, Burton decided to see how far he could go with the "antic disposition" that Hamlet himself puts on. Is Hamlet mad, pretending to be mad, or is Hamlet being played by an actor who is mad? Could he, without changing a word, stretch the emotional contour of the role to the breaking point? He found that no matter what he did—yelling and whispering, talking very fast or absurdly slowly, pausing frequently or never seeming to breathe—the audience loved his performances. What the audience might not have liked would have been an actor who had fallen into a dullness, a dreariness brought on by the boredom that in Burton's case inspired a desperation that served him well.

The point here is that a performance—whether in drama or music—comes alive because the performer is feeling and communicating to the audience more profoundly than merely delivering the text like a parcel. When a musician plays a piece by Mozart, for example, it is not enough to play the notes accurately ("anyone can play accurately"!) but to invest them with meaning. As Burton discovered in his long run as Hamlet, the meaning is not carved in stone even when words are concerned, and in the case of music, "meaning" is much more open to interpretation. Subtext is the emotional context beyond the words that is communicated in drama by the actor's inflection, timing, vocal tone and volume, and physical expression.

In written music, we already have the pitch (inflection), timing, and dynamics as notated on the page, but the performing musician still must invest the gestures with an emotional subtext. This is often referred to as "saying something with the music." In the following exercise, the idea is to say something...anything...to engage fully with the concept of subtext in musical performance.

This exercise is for performers.

1. Play a musical phrase (from a piece of standard repertoire) cleanly, accurately, without rubato or much expression, keeping the dynamics to a mezzo forte throughout. In other words, play it as if it bored you.
2. Play the same phrase as if you hated the music and are being forced to play it by an evil taskmaster.
3. Play the same phrase as if it were a secret signal between you and your beloved, suggesting in musical code a location where you will meet later this evening in the moonlight, unknown to anyone else.
4. Play the same phrase as if you were from another planet where they play a completely different sort of music and this phrase seems incomprehensible to you.
5. Play the same phrase as if you think you are the greatest practitioner of your instrument alive today and are sure everyone agrees with that assessment of your abilities.
6. Play the same phrase timidly, as if you are unsure if you deserve the honor of playing such great music.
7. Play the same phrase as if you love the music, identify with the composer's emotions and point of view, and feel that it expresses exactly your thoughts on the subject of...(fill in the blank.)

EXTREME PHRASING (RICHARD BURTON'S HAMLET)

Using a text from a play or novel, perform it out loud with extreme changes every sentence or clause: whisper one phrase, scream the next, read at high speed the next, then read very slowly, then insert lots of pauses, then read with widely varied inflection.

Now that you have tried it with a text, **choose a piece of music to perform in this manner.** Each musical phrase is to be performed with a new element introduced, such as dynamics, articulation, tempo change, rests and fermatas, a cadenza, etc.

Play each phrase in a manner similar to the speaking example above. Keep the energy moving forward toward the final cadence.

The four examples below are suggestions only. Feel free create your own extreme readings as you go.

Remember that dynamics are not merely about volume, but also about character. Decide if *ppp* will be hushed and nervous, quiet and tender, soft and secretive, or whatever else you may think of. *Why* should a phrase get faster and louder? Is it fear, anger, ecstasy, or what? Why would you play a phrase *staccato* or with *sforzandi*?

1. Play the first phrase *ppp* and legato.
2. Play the second phrase faster and louder.
3. Play the third phrase extremely staccato.
4. Play the fourth phrase riddled with sforzandi.

This exercise is bound to release some pent-up energy and will give the performer the feeling of being free and wild!

ROBOTO/RUBATO

This is a performance exercise for either a solo player or an ensemble.

1. Choose any piece of music you know and can play.
2. Imagine you are a robot performing this work. You've been programmed to play the work so that everything on the page is represented, but you have no feelings, cannot be emotional, and can only play in absolutely strict metronomic time.
3. You are no longer the robot, and you play the same music again, but this time every moment must be somehow human. Nothing should sound like the robot's performance.
4. Alternate phrases playing as a robot and a human.

SUGGESTION: Notate (using dynamics, tempo markings, and articulation marks) all the elements that made the performance sound human rather than robotic. What does the page look like now compared to the original?

REMOTE CONTROL (ROBOTO II)

This exercise requires a minimum of two people.

One person holds a remote control (a phone or similar device is fine, or it can be an imaginary device). The other person is ready to play an instrument.

The instrumentalist is a robot that has been programmed to respond to the remote control. The remote device can control the following: *crescendo; diminuendo; staccato; legato; piano; forte*; pedal (for a piano); *tremolo* (string instrument); *pizzicato* (strings); tempo and *accelerando/rallentando*.

The instrumentalist starts playing a piece and after a few phrases, the person with the remote uses the device to alter parameters of the piece. In order to do this, the person with the remote points the device at the robot musician, presses the button, and says *"Crescendo!"* or *"Staccato!"* or *"Accelerando!,"* etc. The performer must immediately do what the remote requires, adding each new parameter to the last. The person controlling the remote can also *undo* a command. *Staccato* is canceled out by *Legato*, but you can also alter/cancel more than one parameter at a time, by issuing commands such as *"Staccato* and *crescendo!"* or *"Legato, accelerando, crescendo!"* It is important that the person with the remote be reasonable in their demands so that the player can actually make it happen.

This exercise can free up an interpretation because all the interpretive choices are random and because those random choices are controlled by someone other than the performer. After this exercise, when the performer returns to playing the piece in a normal manner, all the choices will be understood more vividly, and a fresh approach should be possible.

IMPROMPTU SONATA

This is an extremely difficult exercise and can be achieved only by very advanced pianists who can already improvise with confidence and skill, and who have good memories. The point here is to challenge a group of proficient improvising pianists and give them a rare opportunity to do something together (pianists live a notoriously singular existence.) The exercise provokes conversation about sonata form and also about compositional issues in general.

Each of four pianists is assigned a part in the sonata design, as follows:

Pianist I: Group I (or Theme I)
Pianist II: Transition to Group II (a dramatic modulation to appropriate key)
Pianist III: Group II (or Theme II, in the appropriate key)
Pianist IV: Development

It may not be necessary to go past the development, but it would make the exercise more complete and satisfying to do so. Pianists I, II, and III must then play the music of the recapitulation, staying in the tonic. Pianist IV may add a coda. Using the plan described above, the pianists improvise a sonata together.

Note: When I used this exercise at Juilliard, the pianists stood around the keyboard listening and watching closely and as one stood up from the bench, the next sat down to play, trying to make the transition seamless.

VARIATION
An easier version is to use a less complex design, such as variations. Then, one pianist makes a theme, and each successive pianist plays a variation.

SOUNDSCAPE

I have used this exercise with large groups, even entire concert bands and orchestras when I have visited college music departments, and in many cases it has created a new atmosphere for the group, giving a sense of adventure and theatricality to their rehearsals afterward.

The idea is to create a scene from life using instruments, singing, talking, and other sounds. Below are two such ideas. Think of more and try your own.

The Village on a Summer Night

What sounds might we hear on a summer night in a small village or town? Perhaps someone is practicing scales on the trumpet, a dog is barking, people are singing in a tavern, dance music is playing somewhere, people are arguing, a police siren goes by, someone is calling for their dog (the one barking) to come home.

Arrange all the musicians around the rehearsal space so that this scenario can be performed. Perhaps record it and listen to it together, discuss the results and then try it again.

Dickens' London in the Morning

What sounds might we hear in the morning in London during Charles Dickens' lifetime? Street vendors are singing their brief songs ("Strawberries! Sweet and red! Buy my Strawberries!"), horses are riding by (percussion instrument?), a policeman is moving people along, a band is practicing for their lunchtime concert. Arrange all the musicians, as in the exercise above, and create this sonic scene. What else can be added?

When performing these scenes, it may help to let it go on for some time, even if it does not seem to be going well at first. Given time, people loosen up, start to experiment, discover ideas, and react to each other's ideas. Time pressure only impedes the process. If you are game to try this, give it your full attention and plenty of time.

BEETHOVEN THE HEALER

This exercise is for performers, both instrumentalists and singers.

Beethoven understood that music can have healing powers and he often improvised for his friend Antonie Brentáno to ease her suffering. Beethoven also improvised for his former student Dorothea von Ertmann (née Graumann), to whom he dedicated his Piano Sonata in A, op. 101. Unable to weep after the death of her three-year-old son, Frau Ertmann was invited by Beethoven to his home, where he played to her for over an hour until she began to cry, finally able to confront her grief and release her anguish.

In this exercise, imagine that you are Beethoven improvising for Dorothea. Dorothea von Ertmann comes to your home, grief stricken and unable to weep. She sits in a dimly lit room where you are seated at the piano. The purpose of your improvisation is clear: to heal her suffering, to bring her some peace. As you play, listen to your thoughts and imagine her grief. Let the music unfold as you go deeper into this relationship. Do not give up on her. (If you are not a pianist, pick a great artist of your instrument and imagine yourself to be that person.)

WHY ARE YOU PERFORMING?

This exercise is for performers, both instrumentalists and singers. In the Beethoven the Healer exercise above, you had a very specific goal and imagined yourself to be someone else. In this exercise, you have choices for the goal and you perform as yourself. Also, you may either improvise or play an existing piece to achieve the goals of this exercise.

Improvise or play an existing piece while imagining the following situations (below.) Keep the goal of your performance in mind at all times. If you are improvising, fit your music to the situation. If you are playing an existing piece, first consider the situation and then select the music. Your performance, not just selection of the piece, should be influenced by the situations described.

1. You are playing for a friend who is going to have a serious operation tomorrow. Your goal is to calm your friend and give her positive feelings.
2. You are playing for a child who has trouble sleeping. Your goal is to play music to help the child sleep, but a mere lullaby will not be enough. Your music should seem to tell a story, at the same time lull the child into sleep.
3. You are playing for a friend who is about to go on a first date. Your goal is to get your friend, who is very distracted by other things, into a romantic mood.
4. You are playing for a sports team before an important game. They have been on a losing streak, and your performance needs to rally their spirits.
5. For this situation, you must select an existing piece of music rather than improvise. You are playing for a group of music students, a master class. All of the

students are studying the piece you have chosen to perform. Your goal is to reveal the essence of the piece to them. You want them to listen to the music, not to merely judge your playing. You want them to hear it as if for the first time.

MELODIC DREAM—PERFORMANCE VARIATIONS

This exercise should be done in silence, in the mind. However, in a class where there are instrumentalists, it would be interesting for a musician to actually play the exercise described below both before and after it is tried in silence, in the imagination.

- Choose a simple melody, one you know well.
- Hear it played on a familiar instrument—a clarinet, for example.
- Listen to the same melody again played on a clarinet, but this time the player adds ornaments (trills, glissandi, grace notes, etc.).
- Listen to the same melody again played on a clarinet, but this time there are no ornaments, but the player adds interesting dynamics and articulations—a crescendo, a diminuendo, staccato notes, legato phrases, a sforzando, etc.
- Hear the same melody again played on the clarinet, but this time it is played very slowly and quietly.
- Hear the same melody again played on the clarinet, but this time it is played at a very fast tempo and loudly.
- Hear the melody with a variety of dynamics, ornaments, articulation, and tempo changes—allow this to happen as in a dream. Notice when you are manipulating the performance and when it seems to be happening without you.

NICHOLS AND MAY GAME #1

The innovative comedy team of Mike Nichols and Elaine May used to ask their audiences for a first line, a last line, and a style, and then they would improvise a scene within those parameters. Because everyone knew the last line in advance, it was fun to see how the improvisers navigated toward it, and also the audience could tell immediately when the scene was over.

For example, a member of the audience might suggest the first line, "Here, Doctor, is where it hurts." Another audience member then suggests a last line, such as: "Yes, I do have a pet giraffe." And the style? Perhaps Shakespeare, Dickens, Arthur Miller, Alfred Hitchcock, or Jane Austen.

This exercise is modeled closely on the Nichols and May approach described above:

Two musicians, playing any instruments or singing, ask the audience or their classmates for an opening motif or phrase, a final cadence, and a style. There is no need for the suggestions to relate to each other (as you see in the text example above).

The suggested opening might be just a rhythm on one note, a chord progression, a melodic fragment (motif), a Beethoven-like rhetorical gesture, or anything at all. The final cadence could likewise be anything, no restrictions! The two suggestions should be clear, precise, easy to remember. The style suggested could be somewhat general, such as Classical, Jazz, World Music, Country and Western, Rock, or Pop, or—for advanced improvisers—the style could be that of a specific composer or performer, such as Beethoven, Debussy, Schoenberg, Meredith Monk (if doing this with voices), or Art Tatum.

Note: Even with a general suggestion, it may help the improvisers to channel particular composers or performers without telling the audience. Specificity provides clarity.

NICHOLS AND MAY GAME #2

Nichols and May not only did improv comedy using audience suggestions, as described above, but they also kept ideas and lines that worked from those improvs and used them to create scripts that could be repeated.

Using this approach as inspiration, follow up on your improvisation for *Nichols and May Game #1* by keeping two memorable moments and using them as the beginning and ending of a *new* improv. Continue with new improvisations, always adding two phrases from the previous improv as you go. The idea is to keep enough of your own improvised ideas from one to the next that soon you will have a structured piece, like a script, that can be notated and performed exactly as written.

The improvisers could be the same people throughout this exercise or new partners may be chosen for each improv. If possible, record the improvs so that they can be listened to afterward and discussed, and so the phrases to be kept can be notated from the recording.

NICHOLS AND MAY GAME #3

Another improv comedy technique is to start with a familiar quote, perhaps from a play. One actor might say, "To be or not to be/That is the question" and the first improv line from the second actor might be, "If I remember correctly, you live in 2F, not 2B, so kindly take your pet meerkat and leave my apartment."

Why not start your improv with a phrase from a famous piece of music? An equivalent idea to quoting from Hamlet, as above, might be to start with the dramatic opening of Beethoven's Fifth Symphony or the opening of his first string quartet (Op. 18, No. 1). The opening quotation should be a phrase of music that the performers know well and are comfortable reacting to. It can be the first line of a well-known popular song or folk tune or a TV theme song.

Remember that this is a *music* improvisation and there is no need to attempt to be funny, as in improv comedy! Any mood that emerges from the opening quotation is fine to explore. Let it evolve without controlling or forcing.

MUSIC, LTD.

This exercise is based on the concept that limitations help focus the imagination. All games have limitations—boundaries and rules that define what it means to play. In tennis, a serve must not hit the net and it must land within the service box; the server must stand behind the baseline. In chess, each piece may move only in a particular manner. These limitations make it fun and challenging and focus the player's mind. The rules and boundaries define the game itself.

In this exercise, a short list of limitations is given to an improviser by a colleague, members of a class, or by a teacher. Alternatively, the limits may be written on scraps of paper that are put into a hat so that the improviser can pull them out randomly. The number of limitations should vary—there can be just one to start, but when the improviser has had some experience with this, there may be three or four limitations.

Here are some examples of limitations: *the music must be very quiet (ppp); the music must have sudden accents; the music must be very fast; the music must be very slow; the music must be staccato; the music must have repeated notes, etc.*

Before beginning the improvisation, the improviser decides what the given limitations will *mean* or *suggest*. For example, if the limitations are *the music must be very quiet with sudden accents*, the improvisor might decide that this is because the feeling is one of someone sneaking about in the dark, looking for something, and occasionally knocking things over. Or if the suggestion is that the music be very slow, the improviser might decide that this is because the mood is one of grief or, alternatively, that the mood is one of peace and contentment. It is essential to a good improvisation that the limitations be defined in this way so that the performer's imagination is fully engaged.

This game can be played in any style of music, as the limitations do not define or refer to any particular genre. In fact, there is no need for the improvisation to stick to any one style of music, unless that specific limitation is chosen as part of the game itself.

GROUP RONDO

This exercise requires an ensemble of at least three musicians, but a large group is preferred. Any combination of instrumentalists and singers will work for this improv and the music may be in any style. The exercise can even be performed by a full orchestra if there is a conductor prepared to lead the exercise.

First, a theme is chosen that everyone will play in unison. This tune may be in any style and should be a complete theme, but not too long. The tune should be memorized so that there is no reading of sheet music during the exercise.

The structure of this improve is simple and familiar: full ensemble statements of the tune alternate with improvised solos by members of the ensemble.

The solos should not be accompanied so that each soloist is completely free to do whatever she likes. Soloists do not have to improvise on the theme or stick to the mood or the style of the theme. The solos may be wild or tame, comic, tragic, pastoral, scary, or in any mood or several moods; tonal, modal, or atonal; with or without pulse or both. Surprise everyone!

VARIATION
Soloists may continue the idea from the previous soloist or react to it in some way.

About the group theme: A conductor or group leader (from within the ensemble) might indicate that the group theme should be played quietly or loudly, staccato or legato, faster or slower. The length of the solos may be left to the soloist, *or* the group leader or conductor may give a signal to the soloist to come to an end and bring in the group for the theme.

LISTEN CLOSELY

This exercise involves a performer and a group of listeners. A piece of notated music must be used rather than improvised music in order for it to work.

The performer plays several phrases of a piece of music for the group. Then the player performs the same music again but makes two subtle changes (or perhaps not-so-subtle changes). The changes might be pitches, displaced octaves, octave doublings, dynamics, articulation, note(s) added to chords, harmony change, rhythmic alteration, etc. Members of the listening group volunteer to identify the changes. As the game proceeds, the player could make as many as four changes in the music. It is important that the atmosphere should be that of a game, not a test. If a listener can identify all the changes correctly, that person becomes the next player.

Note: It is advisable for the performer to notate the changes into the score, perhaps lightly in pencil (out of sight of the listeners) so that they are repeated exactly. Otherwise the game is not fair. *This sharpens listening skills. What if we always listened to music so carefully?*

STREET SCENE

First, the background story:

When I composed the incidental music for the The Acting Company's production of Goldoni's play *Il Campiello* in 1980, the director, Liviu Ciulei, decided that the music should be played by the actors on stage as street musicians rather than stick with the original plan, which was to record the score with professional musicians. To make this work, I taught a few of the actors to play simple folksy music on a mandolin, ocarina, concertina, and tambourine. Then Ciulei decided to make the street musicians blind. This meant that the actors could no longer look at their fingers when playing, so I had to simplify the music further, which I did by taping up holes on the ocarina, tuning the mandolin to a minor chord, and breaking all but two buttons on the concertina. (I could leave the tambourine as it was.) The result was that the actors played extremely simple music with one chord and a very limited melody.

But the actors were very convincing as a wandering band of blind musicians, and the music had a striking effect due to their ability to connect to the simplest sounds with deep-felt emotion and to project their feelings through their playing, even though they had just learned to play these instruments. That is the story behind this exercise.

This exercise requires an ensemble of at least three players but no more than about six.

The ensemble is a wandering band of street musicians who can only play a few notes on their melodic instruments (flute, violin, trumpet, etc.) and they can only play one chord on their polyphonic instruments (piano, guitar, banjo, accordion, harp, etc.), just as in the theater story described above. Before performing it for listeners, the group should decide

on the mood—sorrowful, joyous, silly, threatening, etc.—
and then select harmonies and notes that will help project
that mood. The performance should be improvised with no
rehearsal. The improvisation should last at least 3 minutes to
be effective.

SILENT MOVIE

When I was a teenager, I had the opportunity to improvise piano accompaniments to silent movies at a pizza-and-bar restaurant in the Adirondacks. Sitting at an upright piano, I had to crane my neck to watch the screen. I followed the action closely, and played whatever popped into my head, often drawing on famous melodies, whether popular songs, TV theme songs, or motives by Beethoven—anything could be recycled to fit the moment. The action dramas were more suited to varied musical improvs than were the comedies, except when there were chase scenes, which occurred in both genres. The music required to support these brief action dramas fell into several melodramatic, stereotyped categories: hero's theme; damsel's theme; villain's theme; threat music; despair music; chase music; fight music; triumph music; love music; celebration music.

There are three approaches to this exercise:

1. If there is a class or group, three or four people stage a "silent movie" while an instrumentalist spontaneously accompanies the performance. To accomplish this, the story should be figured out in advance, characters assigned, and a storyboard written. The instrumentalist (not necessarily a pianist) must have an opportunity to read the storyboard before the improvisation begins. The actors do not speak, but mime their way through each scene.
2. If there is no class or group, the performer writes a storyboard and places it on the piano rack or music stand and improvises the music for the scenes, sticking closely to the moods suggested by the scenario.
3. An actual silent movie is shown (on a computer or any screen available) and musicians take turns improvising

the music in real time. If there are several musicians, each can be assigned a character in the film or a mood/emotion (danger, joy, love, etc.).

If this improvisation is recorded, then it may be used when others are available to react to the music by acting out the storyboard while the recording is played back.

Note: For many people acquainted with traditional silent-movie piano music, there are clichés—tremolos on diminished 7th chords, for example—that will inevitably arise during an improvisation. Nothing is wrong to do. Accept the clichés and enjoy them. At the same time, see what you can do to spice up an old chestnut. Polytonality? Rhythmic surprises? Octatonic theme? Maybe the villain's theme is in a different mode from the others or the chase/fight scene uses clusters!

SAMPLE SALE

A relatively new enterprise in the music world is the sale of samples, loops, and beats. There is a loop-and-beat industry that makes millions for musicians who want to profit from peddling "sample packs" to those looking to integrate ready-made *ostinati* (the old word for *groove*, which predates *loop*) into their own music "productions." A consequence of our digital era, buying and selling sample packs, loops, and beats is extremely common now.

What if this had been technologically possible in previous times? I can imagine Domenico Alberti selling his bass line accompaniment figure (Alberti bass) to composers who could write tunes but not accompaniments or Henry Cowell selling his clusters (Bartók *did* ask for permission to use them!) or Schoenberg selling 12-note rows with ready-made permutations. Bach could have made a fortune selling the pattern from his Prelude No.1 in C Major from Book I of the Well-Tempered Clavier. In fact, Charles Gounod used all of it for his *Ave Maria* and Bach never got a Euro. Was Gounod the first DJ? Hardly. In the 15th and 16th centuries, borrowed melodies were often paraphrased in polyphonic compositions. This is an old tradition!

EXERCISE

1. Select a loop or beat (ostinato or rhythmic pattern) from any composer whose music you admire—from any time or place—and use it as the backdrop to your piece. You can improvise a line over the loop or compose a melody to fit with it. The styles do not have to mesh. For example, use an Alberti bass by Mozart (or

Clementi) and improvise over it in a more modern style. (Poulenc might spring to mind!)

2. Take several phrases by composers you admire and stitch them together (mix it up) in the manner of a DJ to create something that neither of those composers would claim as their own. (Disclaimer: You are legally on your own here! Don't use copyrighted music if you intend to record or perform this in public.)

IV

THE FEELING OF AN IDEA

Musical Dreaming and Thinking

A COMPOSER I INTERVIEWED IN a preconcert talk about his new work remarked to the audience, "I didn't try to think of the idea for this piece, it just suddenly hit me." But isn't that always the way getting an idea feels? This is commonly called the Aha! moment. When we suddenly gain insight, we feel we have solved a problem and an idea appears.

No matter how hard we try to think of an idea, ideas seem to suddenly occur to us. An idea may be simple or complex but the feeling of an idea is always exhilarating. When an idea arrives, it feels like a gift. It may be a solution to a problem we have been pondering, but the idea's sudden appearance feels like a surprise nonetheless. We cannot force an idea into existence. No matter how long we gaze upward to the right, staring at that mysterious point on the ceiling where it seems like we will find an idea, there are none lurking there. To facilitate idea-getting in music, we need to dream in music as well as think about it.

When we dream, we are both the audience of our dream-show and a performer on the dream-stage. In that dream state, in which creativity flows freely, we feel as though we have been given complementary tickets to a box seat at the opera or have been invited to a private screening of a new movie. If we watch and/or listen to the dream-show, commonly referred to as a

The Mind's Ear. Bruce Adolphe, Oxford University Press. © Oxford University Press 2021.
DOI: 10.1093/oso/9780197576311.003.0005

daydream, and if we pay attention, it is likely that an idea will present itself.

Just as in science and math, a musical insight is actually a solution to a problem. In music, the problem may be how to modulate from one mode or key to another in a way that feels new and that fits the dramatic moment, or how to resolve a dissonance in a surprising way or in a way that is exhilarating, or how to create a particular atmosphere or texture using only certain instruments that are available for the music.

Unlike in science or math, a musical solution is a personal choice rather than a fact of nature or a correct answer. And yet a truly inspired personal choice may have the feeling of a universal truth, one that connects to the lived experiences of others, but in a revelatory way, giving listeners the same Aha! moment that the composer experienced when the idea presented itself.

To dream, as I use the word in this book, is to allow an uninterrupted flow of musical events or sonic "images" to appear in the mind's ear. To dream is to be in the music. You might say it is to think in music rather than to think about music.

To think, as I use the word in this book, is to consider the ideas of the dream: to edit, criticize, expand, reorganize, and refine the dreamed ideas.

The musical dreamer is uninhibited ("I can write anything I want!"), technically free from reality ("Who cares if the violin can actually play that passage?"), and inside the musical moment ("What a sensuous harmony!"). As Beethoven said to the violinist Ignaz Schuppanzigh when Schuppanzigh had complained that a particular passage was awkward to play, "Do you believe that I think about your miserable fiddle when the muse strikes me?"

The musical thinker is judgmental ("That is so corny!"), conscious of the limitations of physical reality in musical performance ("The violin cannot really play that!"), and detached from the musical expression ("That harmony is used too often in this passage!").

There is no right or wrong way to combine dreaming and thinking. The two states of mind may function simultaneously in parallel streams, flip back and forth, or operate independently, available to the composer only at separate times. Some composers work out "pre-compositional" plans—strategies, structures, procedures, or maps—that function as boundaries in which their imaginations then play by the rules or break them knowingly.

What about composing in a traditional procedure such as a canon or fugue? Is it possible to "dream" a fugue, unfettered by the technical considerations that define the concept? The answer depends on the level of experience the composer has with the procedure in question. If composing a canon is a new challenge, then the composer has no choice but to think about the technical requirements that make the music a canon while writing. But if the composer is used to working with canons and is familiar with the ins and outs of canonic methods, then yes, the composer can dream musical canons. This is generally true of musical thought: to imagine mixtures of instrumental colors, one must be very familiar with instrumental timbres; to clearly dream harmonic music, one should have experience with harmony, whether it is from playing an instrument capable of harmony or by studying harmony as a separate discipline.

It is not necessary to be able to analyze harmony to dream in it—it is only necessary to have practical experience. For most people this would mean performing, but even attentive listening is enough to allow a certain level of musical dreaming. Performing experience, however, is the most common and usually most direct route to musical dreaming. This is obvious if you play an instrument, because it is typically easier to imagine new music on an instrument you play than on instruments you do not play. However, the ability to imagine music on any instrument or groups of instruments is a facility that can be developed with practice.

Every composer uses a musical vocabulary and the memory of other music as a landscape for musical dreaming. The exercises in this book that address the dreaming/thinking aspects of the musical imagination are designed to stimulate both states and to draw attention to their very existence. How an individual integrates or separates musical dreaming and thinking as part of an improvisational or compositional process is personal, and it is likely that every musician does this differently.

However, many people run into "writer's block," and a very good way to get over this problem is to stop editing and criticizing one's work while trying to get ideas flowing. Separate the process into dreaming and thinking. Dream first, accepting all thoughts as worthy, and only afterward think critically, editing as if someone else had written the music you dreamed.

IMPROVISING AND COMPOSING (I DON'T KNOW WHAT I THINK TILL I HEAR WHAT I SAY)

In real-life conversation, we talk fluently without planning our sentences or even our thoughts. We speak in response to other people without hesitation and may even find ourselves expressing an idea or emotion clearly for the first time, completely spontaneously, unrehearsed. In emotional moments, we may even make a spontaneous, impassioned speech about something, words flowing seamlessly into full sentences, sentences into paragraphs.

But if we were to write down that speech or copy out our conversations, would they make a good scene for a play? Would the speech be worth putting into print? Perhaps, but probably not. Some people may speak spontaneously in full, clear, compelling sentences and paragraphs, but most do not. (The composer Milton Babbitt spoke in full chapters complete with footnotes and neuroscientist Antonio Damasio speaks in elegant prose that borders on poetry in at least four languages.)

Improvisation on a musical instrument is an important skill for all musicians, even those who do not improvise in public as part of their performances. Improvisation engages emotions, challenges technique, and frees the imagination. Much of the music performed by classical musicians had its origin the composer's improvisations and so being in touch with that mindset can illuminate aspects of the music that may seem mysterious otherwise.

In the music of Beethoven, for example, a quiet contemplative passage will suddenly be interrupted by a violent outburst of loud music. This dramatic device was the result of his experiences improvising at the piano before gatherings of members of the aristocracy. We know from letters that

Beethoven loved to lull his listeners into a dreamy, pensive or even mournful mood and then shock them with an unprepared *fortissimo*.

Composition usually entails taking improvised music (whether instrumentally or mentally improvised) as a starting point and then making choices—selecting and eliminating music, elaborating and developing ideas, refining details, and creating a structure—just as telling a story verbally would be only the beginning of the process of writing a novel.

Can one improvise without understanding the musical vocabulary or techniques we are playing? Here is a story, a Russian folk tale that addresses the question above:

An old man with a long white beard was playing with his little granddaughter. The girl asked, "Grandpa, when you sleep at night do you have your beard outside the covers or inside the covers?"

The old man thought about this for a while and to his surprise, he could not recall whether he sleeps with his beard inside or outside the covers. "I will pay attention to what I do with my beard tonight," he told his granddaughter, "and let you know."

That night, the old man stood by his bed, wondering whether he usually puts his beard inside or outside the covers. "I have been doing this every night for many years," he thought, "and yet neither seems right!" Finally, in order to go to bed, he decided to put his beard inside the covers. He could not sleep. He tossed and turned and was very uncomfortable. "Aha!" cried the old man! "Obviously, I must sleep with my beard outside the covers or I would have been able to fall asleep by now." He put his beard outside the covers and tried to sleep. Again, he tossed and turned and was unable to fall asleep. He kept changing his mind all night and became terribly agitated and exhausted. He had a stroke and was found dead in the morning.

A Russian friend of mine assures me that this story is considered funny in Russia.

Clearly, the old man never thought about where to put his beard and yet he put it somewhere every night for years. We will never know the answer to the little girl's question and we will never know if he did it the same way every night either. The point is clear: we often do things easily without thinking and analysis might interfere with our ability to perform relatively simple tasks because it may make us self-conscious. But there is more to consider.

In music, there are many people who improvise freely without "understanding" or analyzing their musical actions. Performers of classical music memorize large, complex scores, and when they perform they often feel as if they are not thinking but rather being or simply doing the music. What does it mean to understand something in music?

All too often, we use the word *understand* in connection with words, as if to understand something means to put it into words. Often in a master class, a famous musician will ask a student musician, "What does this piece mean?" or "What mood are you trying to establish here?" While these questions are perfectly reasonable in some instances, a student's inability to answer these questions does not mean she does not understand the music or have a mood in mind. Simple emotional words— peaceful, agitated, sorrowful, exalted—may only scratch the surface of a musical utterance, and may seem trivial to someone who has been studying and performing a musical work. If music takes us beyond words, why should we think that words are the key to understanding music?

It is possible to understand a piece of music completely on its own terms: sound. Pitch, harmony, rhythm, timbre, articulation, dynamics, shape, texture, energy—these can be understood without words.

Yes, it is possible to use words to illuminate aspects of music—chord names, tensions and resolutions, progressions, nonharmonic tones, structural procedures, and much more—but when a performer communicates through music we can feel that he understands it whether or not he can find words to explain it. I can describe in words the structure of a thirteenth chord and wax poetic about its sensuous dissonance and delicate balance, but it will never be the same as hearing one.

This brings us back to the question of dreaming and thinking in music. The balance between these two ways of relating to music is different with every musician, and changes as our musical experiences form our musical imaginations.

THE SINGLE CHORD IMPROVISATION

It is possible to make a compelling musical statement with only one chord or even a single interval. Consider the pulsating C major chord in the opening phrase of Beethoven's *Waldstein Sonata*, the *Moonlight Sonata*'s mournful arpeggiated C# minor chord, the compelling open fifths that start the Finale of Debussy's Sonata for Flute, Viola, and Harp, or the breathless accompaniment figure in the first half-bar of Mozart's G Minor Symphony no. 40 before the melody appears. In these pieces and countless others, the mood and energy is immediately established with only one chord.

What communicates the mood and energy? Tempo, rhythmic patterns, range, dynamics, texture, resonance, articulation.

This exercise works two ways: in the mind only; using an instrument.

- Imagine a concert hall.
- You are in the audience.
- A soloist appears on the stage
- The soloist begins to play a piece that you feel is very compelling. Perhaps it is sorrowful or joyous, violent or mysterious.
- You realize that the soloist is playing only one harmony—there is nothing else but the one chord and yet the piece speaks clearly to you.
- Listen to the music with full attention.
- Can you play (some of) what you heard? Can you notate it?

VARIATION: A DREAMING/THINKING SCENARIO

In the dreaming part of the exercise, you let the music flow without interruption and without being judgmental or self-conscious.

Dreaming:

You are on stage.

You are the soloist/composer.

Select a single chord. Play it, feel its resonance.

A mood occurs to you. Feel it.

Immediately begin to play the opening phrases of a piece that projects that mood using only that one chord. Keep it going as long as you can. Play freely without hesitation. Stop the moment you feel it is over.

Thinking:

Think about the performance you just gave (described above) and ask yourself if the tempo, dynamics, range, rhythmic patterns, texture, resonance, and articulation worked for the mood. What could you improve? Which element worked best and which needs to be reconsidered? Try to play a few phrases addressing the issues you have raised.

Dreaming:

Now you again play the opening phrases of a piece that project the chosen mood and selected chord. Let yourself be expressive, dramatic.

Question for the Thinker (still you): Did the performance change because of "your" comments and ideas? Was it better?

More Questions: If you were to write this down, what time signature would you use? What tempo marking? What dynamic and articulation would you notate?

BACH AWAY—IMPROVISATION/ COMPOSITION

This exercise requires instrumental skill.

Choose a piece by J. S. Bach that has a clear repeated pattern (such as the Prelude in C Minor from Book I of the Well-Tempered Clavier for pianists or the E Major Partita for violinists, etc.)

Play the first phrase or two as written by Bach.

Play the same phrase(s) three times, each time in a different mode.

(If the phrase is written in E major, you might play it once in E minor, then in the Dorian mode, then Phrygian, etc.)

Free Form 1: Next, play music based on the pattern that uses any of the above modes, perhaps varying the tempo, adding new dynamics and different phrasing. Maybe add surprising accents or a crescendo. Have fun with it; surprise yourself.

Free Form 2: Next, play music based on the pattern as above, keeping the free-flowing dynamics, but move up and down at various intervals, changing aspects of the music as you modulate. For example, you might play the phrase lyrically in Dorian, and then play it staccato in Phrygian up a half-step and make the last note a complete surprise.

VARIATIONS
The variations are endless. Try it every day, and let yourself discover a new twist each time. It doesn't take much to make a significant alteration in the music.

Preludio

FIGURE 4.1 (Bach Away exercise)

For pianists: sustain one voice with a lyrical legato and play the others staccato; play the bass forte and the other parts piano; make the rhythm irregular; play only one hand then follow with the other in imitation.

For other instruments: think of your own variations and embellishments as you play, add accidentals as if it is a game, slide upward in pitch as you go! Important: When you are playing, enjoy everything that happens. Do not be critical but rather enter the zone where you feel completely free. This may take some time, so do not rush it. No notes are wrong—instead incorporate any surprises into the music. Make it work!

After the performance, you can think about what happened:

• What was the shape of the performance?
• Did it seem to evolve or grow or was it stagnant?
• What elements seemed to deserve a listener's attention most?
• What aspects of the improvisation are worthy of selection for a composition?
• Were certain phrases, modes, dynamics, or articulations more effective than others?
• Did the performance enter a zone where it sounded emotionally charged or free?

Using the improvisation by the Dreamer and the comments of the Thinker, write out a version of the improvisation as a composition.

REMIXING DREAM: AN EXERCISE IN MEMORY AND IMAGINATION

This exercise does not require any technology or equipment for remixing, just your brain.

- Get into a comfortable position for listening to music.
- Conjure up a piece of music you know well.
- Listen to it in your mind.
- While you are listening to this, another piece of music you know appears in your mind.
- Listen to both at the same time, as if you were receiving two radio stations at once.
- Hear one piece louder than the other, and then switch the volume.
- Perhaps it is easier to go back and forth between the two pieces than to hear them simultaneously. If so, let the pieces alternate.
- Let the pieces mix together, blend, separate.
- Let the instruments or voices change places or mix.
- If only a phrase from each piece appears, that's fine—enjoy the fragment and let it evolve.

Note: It may be helpful to hear each piece (or song or phrase) individually before trying to mix them.

It is so easy to mix sounds using technology, but much more challenging using only the mind. However, amazing things can happen spontaneously to the music in your imagination that simply cannot happen spontaneously using technology.

The longer you spend with this exercise, the more remarkable the imagined events will become. Let it go on long enough to feel like a dream about two pieces of music. When it feels like a dream, your imagination is in full swing. Dream—but pay attention!

If you feel that you could not do this exercise, or that it was very difficult, do it again when you are very relaxed, perhaps even sleepy. Enjoy what happens, do not try to make it work or manipulate the sound. You might really listen to recordings of the music earlier in the day to help stimulate your imagination later, when you do the exercise.

HIDING IN BEETHOVEN'S MUSIC ROOM (A DREAM)

When I was a student at the Kinhaven Music School in Vermont, I found myself in the living room of the main house, where the best piano was located, past the hours that were allowed for students. I heard Mr. D enter the room. (Mr. D was the nickname for David Dushkin, founder of the school and brother of the violinist Samuel Dushkin, for whom Stravinsky wrote his *Violin Concerto* and the *Duo Concertante*). I hid behind a large stuffed chair and listened to Mr. D play Brahms on the piano. It was a great experience because he did not know anyone was listening, and he played for himself alone.

What if we got to hear Beethoven or Chopin play as they played when they thought no one was listening? Might they improvise new passages in their established masterpieces? Might they recompose parts of a work and explore new possibilities?

DREAMING
Imagine you were on a tour of the homes of famous composers. You are standing in Beethoven's music room, near his piano when suddenly all the other visitors disappear and you hear footsteps coming up the stairs. The doorknob turns. You quickly find a place to hide—behind a big, stuffed chair or in a closet behind some coats. Beethoven sits down at the piano and begins to play.

Listen to Beethoven as he plays one of his own sonatas—but he is changing it, improvising, stopping and starting over, modulating to a new key, altering dynamics, speeding up and slowing down in startling ways. Keep listening.

VARIATION I
Instead of Beethoven, listen to any great composer-performer, but stay hidden! Chopin should not know you are there!

VARIATION II

This time, when you dream that you are hiding behind some furniture, imagine that you are hearing one composer playing music by some other composer. For example, how would Chopin play through Mozart's music? Would he add embellishments? Change the harmonies? How would Gershwin play through a Bach prelude? What might happen to the rhythm? (This exercise relates directly to my own *Piano Puzzlers* on public radio's Performance Today, where I put two composers together in one piece. I always learn a lot about both composers, about music, and about myself doing this exercise.)

THINKING

After dreaming this exercise a few times with different composer-performers, think about what you heard while hiding behind the sofa. Remember some of the unusual moments. Replay these moments in your mind and describe what happened in the music. If you can, write some of it down.

TALKING, EDITING

Pick an interesting topic or an experience shared by people in the room.

Two people discuss the topic or experience in a completely natural, undirected, uninterrupted conversation—this conversation should be recorded. The conversation should go on long enough that the participants become relaxed and unselfconscious.

- Play back the recording and write it down.
- Edit the conversation to emphasize clarity of ideas.
- Edit the conversation again, this time to emphasize unfocused or wandering aspects of the conversation.
- Edit the conversation to make it a good scene in a play or movie.
- Perform the edited version as if it were a scene in a play.
- Compare the original conversation to the new version.

THE FEELING OF AN IDEA | **141**

MUSICAL TALKING, EDITING

Pick one phrase of music—it can be anything, such as a few bars by Mozart, a folksong, a pop tune, etc.

Two musicians (any two instruments) improvise back and forth on this melodic phrase as if they are having a conversation. For example, the Player I simply plays the phrase unchanged, then Player II plays part of the phrase and adds a new note or two, Player I then plays a musical comment on that phrase by imitating and adding something new. There is no right or wrong way to do this, although it can be done well or not-so-well. What makes it work well is the spontaneity, lack of hesitancy, commitment to the phrase, and (this is very important) emotional engagement. Any phrase can be played with some feeling!

As in the "Talking, Editing" version of this exercise (above), the "dialogue" should be recorded. Then it is played back and notated.

- Edit the improvisation to bring out emotional qualities, leaving out parts of the improvisation that detract from the feeling that emerges.
- Edit the notated version of the improvisation by adding new dynamics and phrasing to what was recorded—improving the "piece" as a composer would refine a sketch.
- Notate the new version to create a final performing edition, and then perform it.
- Compare the original improvisation and the new version.

V

EXERCISES IN COMPOSING

SOME YEARS AGO, AT A summer music festival out west, I was sitting on a porch in the sunshine just outside the large room where the orchestra was in rehearsal. This was a composer's life at its best, sitting on a rocking chair, taking in the crisp mountain air while listening to a rehearsal of my music. (Composers are not usually welcome during the early stages of learning a piece, so the rocking chair just outside was perfectly located for eavesdropping.)

A familiar fellow appeared on the porch and sat in the rocking chair next to mine. After looking at me for a while, he said, "You're a composer, right?"

"Yes," I answered.

"Well," he said, happy to get the opening he needed, "then we both do the same thing: we project abstract thought into a logical format, making it available and real."

Not knowing just how to respond, I answered, "What sort of music do you write?"

"Oh, I don't write music," he smiled. "I design weapons systems."

Defending my position, I quickly said, "I don't think I've ever composed a bomb, but I do hope to bring down the house."

Then I added, "And I look forward to performances of my creations, and I'm guessing you don't look forward to yours."

But his point was that abstract thought was the same creative process no matter toward what end, music or destruction.

The Mind's Ear. Bruce Adolphe, Oxford University Press. © Oxford University Press 2021. DOI: 10.1093/oso/9780197576311.003.0006

Both of us imagined something new, wrote out its design so that it could be built or performed—or made "available and real," as he had said. But composing should bring people together to experience drama, beauty, and at some level, truth.

Truth? What is that? As Keats wrote in "Ode on a Grecian Urn":

Beauty is truth, truth beauty, that is all
Ye know on earth, and all ye need to know.

The weapons systems designer was a scientist, and at some deep level he certainly understood the beauty of how things work in nature, and how that beauty is a kind of truth, a truth about our world. His unfortunate task is not the point!

When I talk of beauty in music, I am not talking about it in a mundane sense, and certainly not in the sense of prettiness or loveliness, but rather Beauty as embodied in the relation of the parts to the whole, a sense of proportion, and the aptness of technique to the idea expressed.

When studying a musical work, it is essential to address details, discover how they relate to the larger form, to see connections among phrases and ideas, and to contemplate how the drama of the music resides in the notes and rhythms.

Too often in music theory classes, general concepts are taught apart from any piece of music. Exercises that have divorced the rules from actual composition are then assigned, and these are usually tedious and unmusical, and do not illuminate the process of composition. Then, the student is asked to hunt for evidence of these rules, procedures, and mundane practices in a piece of music, as if analysis were a treasure hunt. This accomplishes little of value. In fact, this process is backward and denies the theory student the meaningful context that makes learning compelling. It is through getting to know some great pieces well, and through attempts at composing, that students will be motivated to study musical issues.

The exercises in this section are useable in private and class composition studies, and in advanced theory classes. By advanced, I mean that the students have a working knowledge of harmony, are familiar with a variety of composers' styles, and—most importantly—have some writing experience. However, there are times when shock therapy works. Assigning one of these exercises to a class that seems unprepared for it may jolt them into creative action. I have seen it happen. Frequently, students can accomplish a difficult task because it grabs their imaginations and provides a genuine thrill. These same students may still unsuccessfully struggle with a species counterpoint assignment, but I think this says more about the intrinsic value of the exercises than about the students. A classroom full of violinists, cellists, pianists, oboists, and clarinetists will probably not be inspired to learn by doing exercises based on Renaissance choral music they have never sung or heard. Starting with music they know is fundamental to engaging the imagination and inspiring creativity.

Some of the exercises in this section involve imitating masters. It is good for a young composer (and for an advanced theory student) to try to write like a master by imagining herself to be that person. Imitating models is an ancient technique for achieving fluency, precision, and expressivity. It is far better to imitate Brahms or Chopin than to attempt to write "Romantic music" in a general way. To use an augmented sixth chord as Robert Schumann would use it in a phrase of music is an excellent follow-up assignment (for advanced students) to writing the chord in a four-part harmony exercise. To do so confronts the student with a powerful personality, focusing and integrating intuitive and analytical perceptions.

THE NEW SECOND PHRASE

Choose a piece you know well. Leaving the first phrase as is, compose a new second phrase that is stylistically consistent with the first, and yet is totally different from the actual second phrase.

This exercise is effective in many different styles. Try composing a new second phrase for a Beethoven or Mozart sonata, or for an intermezzo by Brahms.

Compose a new second phrase to Stravinsky's *Le sacre du printemps* or to a movement of Ravel's *Sonatine*. Perhaps try writing a phrase in response to the opening of a prelude by Bach.

This exercise has proven very stimulating to students in my classes and is a provocative theory class assignment. It inspires an intuitive reaction at the same time as it motivates analytical thinking.

Interesting questions arise:

- What is the emotional tone of the first phrase?
- What musical ideas dominate the opening?
- How many ways can a composer proceed after a strong first phrase has been composed?
- What expectations—harmonic, rhythmic, melodic, dramatic, structural—are set up in the first phrase?
- Does the first phrase benefit by a contrasting or similar second phrase?
- What elements might change and what might remain the same?

Answering these questions by composing teaches many lessons, more than can be explained by conventional theoretical discussion. By attempting to continue a passage by a composer, one begins to think like that composer, both analytically and intuitively.

First phrase from Beethoven,
Piano Sonata No. 27 in E Minor, Opus 90

FIGURE 5.1 (New Second Phrase exercise with Beethoven, Piano Sonata No.
27 in E Minor, Opus 90)

REVERSE SUBTEXT

For an actor, the subtext is what characters are really thinking and feeling when they say a line. Take the line, "Hi, Honey, I'm home!" The subtext might be any of these: "I'm so tired and very glad to be home"; "Tonight we have a big date!"; "I'm so sick of my life"; "I'm so angry at you!"

Exploring the idea of subtext in music is challenging, since music is not saying one particular thing that can be translated into words. However, by reversing the process, we can experiment, as follows:

- Take a line from a play or make up a line of text.
- Say the line different ways, giving it different subtexts.
- Pick one line reading that seems convincing.
- Write the words on paper, adding rhythmic notation that reflects the reading.
- Add dynamics and articulation markings.
- Give the line, now notated with rhythms, dynamics, and articulation, to someone to read who did not hear you read the line.
- Does the notation convey everything you hoped it would?
- Does the new line reading from your musically annotated text sound as you expected?
- Does the new line reading have the subtext you had in mind?

VARIATION
Do the same exercise, but add one more step: substitute musical notes for the words. Now you have a musical phrase based completely on the subtext.

FOUND IN TRANSLATION

This exercise requires compositional experience and skill. In this exercise, a piece is "translated" into words and then "translated" back into music to get a new piece.

> Listen to a few phrases of a piece of music (live performance or a recording are both fine.)
>
> In words, describe the shape, texture, range, dynamics, articulations, energy, and emotional qualities of the music with as much detail as possible. Do not include names of notes, chords, or any specific technical aspects of the music. When you feel you have a clear description of the music (not a theoretical analysis), write it down.
>
> Using your written description as a guide, compose music without using any actual musical material from the piece you described.
>
> Compare your piece to the original work.

While one person may do this exercise, there is an advantage to doing it with two. If two people with good compositional skills do the exercise together, each person should write a description of music that the other person does not listen to, and so the description is the only guide to composing.

VARIATION

Another way to do this exercise would be to compose three completely different versions of a short verbal description of a musical moment. For example, write three musical manifestations of these words: a violent moment is followed by a soft, pleading gesture, and then there are several violent gestures followed by a quiet, sorrowful melody.

The words above suggest mood, dynamics, texture, and energy, but the notes and rhythms that are used could be in any style. It could be a description of music by Mozart or Beethoven as much as music by Bartok, Schoenberg, or Ligeti.

A variation on this variation would be to compose three different versions of the same verbal description and write each version in the style of a famous composer. How would Beethoven write a violent chord and a soft, pleading gesture? How would Schoenberg do the same? What would Stravinsky compose for this exercise? And finally, what would you write to make it your own?

THOUGHTS
Certainly, music cannot be translated into words or any other media. Whatever music may mean, its meaning is completely bound up in the specifics of sound—notes, rhythms, timbre, texture, energy. Even when we have described music in words that are clear, precise, and vivid, the description is at best provocative. With that in mind, it is instructive (and amusing) to attempt to re-create music that has been described. It is an impossible task to do "correctly" but it can be done well.

CUT, PASTE

This exercise requires compositional ability.

To begin, you need two short contrasting musical ideas. They may be original or taken from an existing piece of music, or perhaps only one of the ideas is original. An idea may be a simple musical gesture, a single-line motif, a few chords, or a rhythmic pattern. The ideas should not be vague but rather clear, vivid, and emotionally charged.

Let's call the ideas A and B. Once you have an A and a B that you like, the first task is to write two separate small pieces of music, one based only on A and the other based only on B.

Next comes the cut-and-paste part: splice the two pieces together so that there is an emotional dialogue between the two pieces.

For Example:

Perhaps the music of A starts in short phrases, only a measure at a time, and is interrupted by B, which begins with longer phrases. Then A grows in phrase lengths while B shrinks. Maybe at the very end, we hear A and B together in some way.

At first, do not concern yourself with the phrases of A and B "fitting together" or connecting, but rather allow them to interrupt each other as unchanged phrases from the original A and B.

After you have a structure based on the interplay of A and B, look at the connecting points to see if changing dynamics, register, or even pitches would improve the music.

Do you know any music that relates to this procedure? Listen to the third movement ("Heiliger Dankgesang") of Beethoven's String Quartet no. 15, opus 132; listen to Bartok's String Quartet no. 4, first movement. Many of Stravinsky's works are composed in this manner.

CONFLICT RESOLUTION

Improvise or compose two phrases of music: the first phrase in one style, the second phrase in a contrasting style. (For example, the first phrase might be Romantic and the second might be Jazz.) How can these two phrases be made into a cohesive piece of music? Should the styles be combined? Should they remain in conflict?

A player or ensemble may approach this as an improvisation, or it may be a compositional challenge to be notated fully before a performance takes place. If it is to be an improvised duet or larger ensemble improvisation, the members of the group might meet to discuss the possibilities, or they can dive right in without preparation.

More Examples: First phrase is a folk tune/second phrase is atonal; first phrase is in a dance rhythm/second phrase has no obvious pulse; first phrase is declamatory, recitative-like/ second phrase has an ostinato (groove or loop).

VARIATION

If there are two or more players in this exercise, there can be "teams" for each phrase: Phrase One Team and Phrase Two Team. In one scenario, each team tries to convince the other to join them in playing its phrase (and musical style). This can lead to a variety of dramatic solutions, including the two teams switching styles and phrases at the end. What are some other endings for the scenario? Try a few possibilities.

THOUGHT

Compositionally, this exercise is perfect for the creation of a score that integrates traditional precise notation with graphic notation to indicate improvisation. Let your dramatic idea for the piece determine the notational style for the score.

METER MADE

This exercise should be done using a pencil and music paper. Computer music notation programs will not work for some of the steps and in general will make this exercise more complicated to do.

Select a piece of music that is all in one time signature. This exercise works well with music by Haydn, Mozart, and Beethoven, but it can be done with any music that is in one time signature, including popular songs. Waltzes and mazurkas by Chopin or marches by Sousa also work particularly well. Use only a single line of the music—such as the violin part to a quartet movement or the melody of a song—or one line of a piano piece, or even a part from an orchestral score.

Copy out several phrases of the music without any time signature and without bar lines. Feel free to remove rests and change note values. Don't be shy! Make a few quarters into eighths, remove a dot, add a dot, create a triplet where there was none before! Add a rest if it makes it more interesting. Treat the melody as an ordered series of pitches only—raw material for your rhythmic ideas.

Next, imagine the music with accents in different places than in the original. (If there were no written accents in the original, then the accents would have been determined by the meter and bar lines, which you have removed.)

Notate accents in new, interesting places throughout the music you have copied.

Now draw slurs that create new phrases (shorter, longer than the original phrases), reflecting your own rhythmic vision of the notes. Let a new rhythmic scheme emerge. Forget about staying in one time signature.

Now draw in new bar lines that reflect the accents and phrases you created.

Put in new time signatures that clearly project the rhythms of your newly crafted melodic line. The accents you add may create yet another layer of rhythmic interest.

Perform the new version of the piece. Play it for someone who knows the original piece and ask if they recognize it. (When the rhythm is changed, even a very familiar piece of music may be unrecognizable.)

THOUGHTS

What music do you know that shifts meters frequently? Listen to Stravinsky's *Le sacre du printemps* (The Rite of Spring), *Les noces* (The Wedding), or *L'histoire du soldat* (The Soldier's Tale). Listen to Copland's *Appalachian Spring* or his Piano Sonata. After listening to some of these pieces, listen to a Chopin waltz. How does meter affect you as a listener?

FIGURE 5.2 Chopin Prelude No. 4 with new rhythmic design (Meter Made exercise)

TIMING!

There is an old joke that goes:

> Comedian: *Ask me what the secret is to my success.*
> Audience member: *What is the secret to . . .*
> Comedian *(interrupting)*: *Timing!*
> Audience member: *your success?*

Interruption is a dramatic device that works in any style of music, and it is a defining characteristic of the Classical style, an essential compositional stratagem in "sonata form" as practiced by Haydn, Mozart, Beethoven, and Schubert. Interruption is a useful technique in improvisation as a way to take the music in a new direction. It is also a strategy than can be used in the exercise "Conflict Resolution."

Exercise:

1. Write a complete tune.
2. Pick a moment in the tune to interrupt.
3. Improvise various interruptions and return to the tune after the interruption.
4. Select one of the improvised interruptions and notate it.
5. Use the tune and its interruption as the basis for a longer musical structure.
6. Write a tune in one style and interrupt it with music in a contrasting style.
7. Perform a tune in one tempo and interrupt it with music in a different tempo.
8. Perform a tune in one dynamic and interrupt it with music in a different dynamic. (Try it with articulation, too: staccato music interrupts legato music. Or a combination: slow, quiet, legato music is interrupted by fast, loud, staccato music. Then what happens?)

GUT FEELING (ACTING OUT)

This exercise is based on a method for discovering emotionally compelling motifs that I discovered for myself while composing a dramatic work. Since many of my pieces are based on stories, I now take this approach often:

- First, I imagine a character's emotional reaction to a situation in the story.
- Second, I take on the role of that character and *physically act out* the scene in order to feel the energy of the emotion *as a distinct rhythmic and dynamic motif.*
- Third, I notate the emotional motif (in rhythm notation and with dynamics).

    Here are two approaches to this idea:

A) Remember an emotional moment from your life (this could be as simple as tasting something delicious, cutting your finger, or being afraid in the dark. Or it might be a more intense memory—anything vivid will do.)
    OR
B) Choose an emotional moment from a story or news event.

Then:

- Act out the moment in pantomime. Do it several times to refine it until you feel you have a convincing reenactment. You might make a video of this moment.
- Observe the energy of the pantomime and identify its rhythm and dynamics.
- Notate the rhythm and dynamics of the emotional moment. This is your motif.

- Choose pitches for the motif.
- Perform the motif on an instrument.
- Write a variant of the motif.

You now have a possible opening of a composition that has a strong dramatic profile. Write several phrases continuing this idea.

GROUP COMPOSING GAME

This exercise requires a group of at least four people who can read music, notate pitch and rhythm properly, and who are familiar with the use of dynamics and articulation. At least some members of the group should be performers.

Everyone in the group needs a sheet of blank music manuscript paper.

1. Each person writes twenty notes on the manuscript paper. These notes should not have any rhythmic value (they are note-heads without stems) and there should be no indication of articulation, phrase groups, or dynamics.

After writing the notes, everyone passes the paper to another member of the group.

2. Each person takes the page of twenty notes written by someone else, and using a staff below writes a rhythmic version of the same notes in the same order. (There does not need to be a time signature, but there may be. Simply choosing note values and applying them to the twenty notes is enough. Adding a fermata—or a few— is also a possibility.)

After writing a rhythmic version of the twenty notes, everyone passes the paper to another member of the group—but not back to the person who wrote the notes! It is best if each phase of this exercise is done by a person new to the "piece."

3. Each person takes the page of rhythmical notes written by someone else, and adds articulations—legato, staccato, accents, tenuto marks, etc.

After adding the articulations, everyone passes the paper to another member of the group. If there are four people, this pass will complete the cycle.

4. Each person in the group takes the page of rhythmical notes with articulation added, and adds dynamics— *pp, p, mp, mf, f, ff, sfz, sffz, fp, crescendo, diminuendo.* After adding the dynamics, everyone passes the paper to the person who wrote the twenty notes on the page.

5. Now members of the group should perform all the completed twenty-note pieces. The pieces may be sung (perhaps with the help of a piano or other instrument) or performed on any appropriate instrument. Everyone should see the final result before it is performed.

DISCUSSION

After the performances, there may be a discussion of the compositional issues raised by this exercise:

Did the original twenty notes (in each case) seem to suggest a musical style, a key, a mode?

Did the rhythms added seem to fit well with the notes or did the rhythms perhaps suggest a surprising take on the notes?

Did the rhythms emphasize tonal areas or range, such as highest and lowest notes?

Did the articulations seem natural or arbitrary to what was already on the page?

What did the articulations and dynamics do to the feeling of the music?

Did the articulations and dynamics bring out expressive possibilities or did they seem superimposed?

Did the articulations and dynamics make it harder to perform? More interesting?

CODA

Each person who wrote the original twenty notes might take his or her finished piece and, after making a copy, edit it by removing or changing any aspect of it that they think will improve the piece. Perform these newly edited versions and compare them to the original group compositions.

IMAGINING A NEW WORK
BY BEETHOVEN

- You are at a concert in Vienna in a room used for intimate performances.
- It is 1821.
- Picture the room, the other audience members.
- See what they are wearing. Hear the hushed conversation (which is in German, whether or not you understand it).
- Beethoven enters and announces that he will improvise at the keyboard.
- Choose the mood and the key.
- Hear the piece following closely as the form freely unfolds.
- Hear the modulations, dramatic pauses, flashes of inspiration, sequences, transitions, repetitions, and surprises.
- Go to a piano and play the opening phrase, or more if you can.
- Write it down.

NEW TUNES FOR OLD SONGS

Write a new melodic line, ignoring the words, for a song by Schubert or Brahms, leaving the piano part as is.

VARIATION

Using a strophic song by Schubert or Brahms, turn it into a through-composed piece by composing music for verses other than the first. Be stylistically consistent and continue to explore the musical ideas of the first verse.

VARIATION

Add a line for violin, clarinet, or oboe to a song by Schubert, Brahms, or Wolf. Do not betray the intent of the composer. Read the text carefully.

Of course, this can be done with any composer. Try it with a song by Debussy or Britten, for example.

From Schubert's "Gute Nacht" (first song in *Die Winterreise*)

A new tune for the same accompaniment:

FIGURE 5.3 (New Tunes for Old Songs exercise)

SLIDING AROUND

Orchestrate a glissando the way various composers would, without actually referring to their works. It should be a long, full orchestral glissando, a beginning or an ending.

Orchestrate a glissando as:

- Stravinsky
- Lutoslawski
- Elliott Carter
- Debussy
- Ravel
- Webern
- What are the issues raised by this assignment?
- Perhaps it may help to imagine a piece by the composer in question (a piece you are making up in his style), which then leads to a glissando.
- Now that you have tried this, orchestrate a glissando your own way.
- Is it harder or easier to do this your own way?

TRANSFUSION

Analyze a musical work you admire. Determine its general structure and significant details. Take note of the dynamics and dramatic shape.

Compose a new work that closely follows the structure, dynamics, dramatic shape, and even the significant details of the work studied. Your work does not have to be in the style of the model at all. (I sometimes do this exercise just for fun. It can yield hilarious results, but it can also be a profound learning experience to take the bones and flesh of a composition but infuse your own blood! My own paraphrase, or parody, of Mozart's *Eine kleine Nachtmusik* is called *I'm Inclined to New Music* and my fantasia for string quartet based on Gesualdo's madrigal *Moro, lasso* is called *More or Less*.)

Opening 10 bars of Beethoven, Piano Sonata Opus 10, No. 1

Allegro molto e con brio

Transfusion (keeping everything but the notes!)

FIGURE 5.4 (Transfusion based on Beethoven, Piano Sonata Opus 10, No. 1)

Opening phrase of Brahms, Sonata No.1 for Cello and Piano in E Minor, Op. 38

Transfusion

FIGURE 5.5 (Transfusion exercise based on Brahms, Sonata No. 1 for Cello and Piano in E Minor, Op. 38)

ARRANGING A FOLK TUNE

Listen to one or two of Benjamin Britten's folk song arrangements.

Listen to one or two of Beethoven's folk song arrangements.

Listen to Luciano Berio's piece *Folksongs*.

Pick a folk song you like and arrange it for voice and piano as if Beethoven, Britten, or Berio were doing it.

Try it as if Brahms were doing it. Try it as Ravel, Gershwin, or Stravinsky.

Now, how would you do it if you were to call it your own?

IS IT OVER YET?

One way a composer can keep a piece of music going is to create a series of deceptions*. In this exercise, use a familiar tune and alter its cadences so that they do not come to a satisfying end, but instead are deceptive in a variety of ways.

Example: Take *Twinkle, Twinkle Little Star* and keep it going for as long as possible with unexpected cadences.

*See the essay DECEPTION IS A GOOD THING (IN MUSIC, THAT IS), above.

A B A OR A A+ A?

Ternary form (ABA) is one of the most common of all musical structures. Inspector Pulse, the "private ear" I invented for the Chamber Music Society of Lincoln Center's family concert series, mistakenly thought that the letters ABA were grades, and so he thought that he would remedy the situation and rewrite the "B section" to make it an "A+ section." He also wrote B sections for tunes that did not have one at all (such as *London Bridge Is Falling Down* and *Happy Birthday*). Why not try this yourself? Write a new B section for any song you know and make it an A+. And then, for a tune that has no B section at all, write your own. Soon the grade point average of many tunes will be vastly improved!

Hint: Ways to "improve" the B section could be to increase the tune's range and harmonic interest. Maybe it should modulate! As for writing a brand-new B section for a tune that lacks one, consider the signature rhythmic and melodic patterns of the A section and base your B section on those, but give them an unexpected twist.

BE SHOSTAKOVICH!

A talented young composition student of mine, who usually wrote several pages a week, had slowed down considerably and was proceeding at the alarming rate of one measure a week.

"I don't know what to write next. I like the opening, but I don't know what the next part should be," he told me.

I could have made several suggestions for his piece, as I often do, or even composed some phrases for him, as I had done in the past, but it would not have really helped him in the long run. I happened to know that the student was fond of Shostakovich.

So, I said, "You may not know what to do, but I'll bet Shostakovich would know. Why don't you pretend to be Shostakovich this week and see what he would come up with to follow what you've written?"

His eyes lit up. Like an actor given a great role, he was eager to get to work. He knew that being Shostakovich would magically give him insight and inspiration, and even the feeling of the experience that he himself lacked.

The idea of this exercise is to temporarily be a composer you admire.

Compose some music *as* that composer rather than *like* that composer. If you are doing this for real, you will know it. (See the Piano Puzzler Preparation section at the end of this book for more exercises related to this one.)

COMPOSE YOUR OWN LEITMOTIF

In Wagner's operas, characters and concepts are assigned musical identification tags, known as leitmotifs. This is different from a "theme song" for a media celebrity or TV show. The leitmotif captures the essence of the character: the energy, the rhythm, the quality of the soul.

What if you had a leitmotif that clearly stood for some essential aspect of your personality? What if instead of a calling card, you presented your leitmotif?

Try to compose your own leitmotif.

VARIATION

Compose a leitmotif for a person you know well. This might be a good way to warm up for composing your own.

Remember: a leitmotif is not a developed piece or a song, but a phrase. It may be brief but it must capture the intended qualities.

SUGGESTION

If everyone in a class writes a leitmotif, then it might be fun to play them without identifying the composers. Then, the class should guess which leitmotif represents which of their colleagues.

Another follow-up idea is to weave the various leitmotifs into an overture or tone poem. If this is accomplished it will be an unforgettable experience for the participants, and far more meaningful than writing a "class song."

Keep a notebook of everyone's leitmotif. Years later, it will be a rare kind of scrapbook: a glimpse back in time into everyone's musical imagination.

VI

PIANO PUZZLER PREPARATION

INTRODUCTION

THE *PIANO PUZZLERS* segment has been a weekly feature on public radio's Performance Today, hosted by Fred Child, since 2002. As I write this chapter, there are about 600 piano puzzlers in my computer. This section is a response to the many music teachers in the piano puzzler audience who have suggested that I create some fun teaching materials based on the puzzlers.

I learn something from every piano puzzler I compose because each has its particular problems to solve. For this edition of *The Mind's Ear*, I have organized the fundamental issues posed by piano puzzlers into a series of exercises culminating in the creation of a piano puzzler. These exercises are necessarily for pianists and composers who play the piano and require a working knowledge of modes, harmony, and other compositional vocabulary and grammar. All of the exercises may be approached as improvisations and/or compositions to be notated. Trying both methods is recommended.

One of the most intriguing aspects of the piano puzzlers is how attentively the audience listens to them. Because they want to identify the mystery composer, they listen for clues to help them: melodic contour, rhythmic profile, harmonic palette, level of dissonance, texture, and much more. While the primary goal of the exercises below is to utilize the vocabulary and grammar of a composer's style, a side effect is an improved ability to listen analytically.

The Mind's Ear. Bruce Adolphe, Oxford University Press. © Oxford University Press 2021.
DOI: 10.1093/oso/9780197576311.003.0007

In order to compose a piano puzzler (in which a popular song, folk tune, show tune, etc., is recomposed in the style of a classical composer), one should be able to reimagine a melody from various perspectives. The penultimate exercise in this book, Be a Private Ear, provides a detailed checklist of the main compositional features that go into composing a piano puzzler. The Private Ear Checklist is a kind of shopping list that reminds you of what ingredients you need to cook something that Chopin, Brahms, Debussy, or Stravinsky might prepare.

The following exercises are based on the parameters mentioned above and address the essential compositional concepts behind the puzzlers through improvisation at the keyboard. These are musical "stretches" and warm-up exercises that will *tone* your compositional muscles and make you ready for stylistic adventures that you can try on your own. Once you have tried an exercise, try it again. Try another one and then go back to the first exercise. It may seem challenging at first, but with repeated efforts it will become easier. It is like musical yoga. It is not a test you take once, but a practice you can use regularly. The final exercise culminates in composing a piano puzzler.

After trying each of these exercises below, ask yourself if any of your improvisations reminded you of a particular composer. If so, try it again but this time with a more conscious effort to imitate that composer.

PIANO PUZZLER PREPARATION EXERCISES

MAJOR/MINOR

Play a well-known, major-mode melody (i.e., *London Bridge Is Falling Down*) as it usually goes, without changing anything about it, in the treble, while playing a chordal accompaniment in minor—not necessarily in *one* minor key, but with chords that come from various minor keys. You can forget about *key* altogether and just play minor chords that fit the tune—mix-and-match.

Note: The melody notes can now be any part of the chord; what was a fifth can be a root or a ninth. Have fun and don't stop to fix anything! Try this with one more than one melody. Notate a version you like.

WHAT'S IN THE PHRYG?

Play a well-known, simple tune (a folk song works well for this) but change the mode; no accompaniment for the first time through. Next, play it again in the same mode adding harmonies from that mode. Play the tune several times, each time using another mode; each time, play it first without accompaniment and then with accompanying harmonies. (Example: *Skip to My Lou* in Phrygian, Lydian, and Mixolydian.)

Note: It is more interesting, and you will get more out of this exercise, if you stay with the same tonic note as you change modes rather than use to the "white-key mode" approach.

VARIATION

Allow the mood of the mode to inspire your improvisation—add embellishments to the melody; find a rhythmic pattern for the accompaniment; pick a tempo that seems to project the mood of the tune in each mode. It is probably good to use a slow tempo to start.

OCTATONIC IMPROV

Play a well-known simple melody (folk song, popular song, etc.) in the octatonic mode. To work out harmonies for this, remember that triads and 7th chords are available on each note of the "tonic" diminished 7th chord when the scale starts with a half-step.

Thinking of music by Stravinsky or Messiaen may be helpful. Ravel and Debussy also used the octatonic mode so they, too, can be your guides in this exercise. If improvising in the octatonic mode is too difficult at first, think of it as a composition exercise and notate it. You may end up with a piano puzzler . . . take your time!

METER MIXUP

Play a well-known tune in a different meter (i.e., play a tune that is usually in 2 in 3 or 5, or other meters). The left hand can keep the meter clear while you freely adapt the tune to the meter. No need to keep the melody in its original rhythmic form (that would necessitate playing some challenging polyrhythms that Stravinsky would have enjoyed). Allow it to fit into the new meter in a naturally flowing way.

FRENZIED PHRASES

Improvise an accompaniment in a wild, frenzied manner with varied rhythmic accents. After establishing this, add a familiar tune in any way that fits. Perhaps the tune is fragmented, and it only appears now and then. Perhaps it appears in sudden bursts of melody, swirling about. Have fun with it! Then, ask yourself: what music do you know that has a frenzied, wild accompaniment? Who wrote that piece?

CHORDS RULE

Improvise a chord progression. After establishing the harmonies, add a well-known tune, freely adapting it to the chords. This may involve changing some notes in the tune or turning notes that were consonant in the original version of the tune into dissonances against the new harmonies. Feel free to write out the chord progression so that you can concentrate on playing the tune in its new environment. If the improvisation goes astray, great. Follow your own lead if it sounds good.

Note: In order to make this work, you might use only the shape and rhythm of the tune, letting the intervals go their own way.

TWO-CHORD MONTE

Play a well-known tune very slowly so that each note has some time to resonate. Next play it again the same way but add unusual, unpredictable harmonies for each note. Try it again, but this time, play *two* harmonies per melody note. Consider that the melody note can be harmonic (part of the chord) or nonharmonic (dissonant to the chord). Eventually, choose some of the chords you like from this improvisation and play the whole thing again but at the normal tempo for that melody. Does your improvisation remind you of a particular composer or style?

A TRILLING TUNE

Play a well-known melody in its pure version. (No accompaniment necessary, but feel free to play one if you like.) Next, add standard ornaments such as trills, turns, and mordents to the tune. Now, play it again but add ornaments wildly, bury the tune in trills, scales, grace notes, and whatever else you devise so it is unrecognizable! Next, play the tune several times in a row while you gradually remove ornaments. Finally, play the tune in its pure state again (but perhaps one ornament returns at the end, like finding sand in your bed after dreaming of the beach).

Note: Ornaments do not have to be Baroque! Feel free to make up your own ornament style.

A TUNE SURROUNDED

Play a well-known tune in the middle register of the keyboard while improvising across the entire range of the keyboard. This can be accomplished in a variety of styles: Romantic arpeggios cascading about, while the tune remains afloat, ringing out in the middle register; pointillistic, jagged comments from all over the keyboard try to distract the tune from its purpose; delicate impressionistic washes of harmony (whole tones, dominant 9th chords) create an ocean of music while the tune cries for help. How do the harmonies fit with the tune? There are many possibilities: sustain certain melody notes so that they ring with the harmonies; play each note of the melody slowly so that each has its own chord; harmonize only every third note of the tune, the others becoming passing tones, etc. (Conjure Liszt, Debussy, Ravel . . . are you writing a piano puzzler?)

DREAMSCAPE

A fun way to start improvising counterpoint is to employ the upper register only, playing imitative phrases between the hands *pianissimo* in a dreamlike texture, using the pedal to create a hypnotic harmonic haze. Pick a well-known tune (another one, please!) and improvise your mysterious and shadowy contrapuntal dream landscape. The tune does not have to be played exactly in its original form, but allow it to bend and twist.

FANTASIA

Here you can bring it all together. Using all the exercises above, improvise a *fantasia* based on a well-known melody (keep the tune simple so you can enjoy the fantasia). The techniques need not appear in the *fantasia* in the order shown above.

Here is a description of a possible fantasia based on exercises above:

The improvisation could start with a quiet contrapuntal dreamscape in the upper register and then the tune appears in a new meter, which gradually becomes ornamented. Perhaps this is followed by a slow, stately version of the tune with unusual harmonies; soon the harmonies wash across the keyboard in arpeggios; now the tune emerges in a new mode, which gives way to a majestic chord progression that builds to a climactic moment when the music explodes into a dynamic, frenzied dance.

FICTITIOUS COMPOSER FANTASIA

Piano puzzlers are always in the style of a famous composer, but what if we wanted to compose a piece in the style of a composer who never existed?

- Imagine a composer from a specific time and place.
- Consider who might be the composer's musical influences. In what ways can we hear those influences in the music and how is the music *not* like those influences?
- Is the composer's music contrapuntal?
- What textures are typical in this music?
- Is the composer's music lyrical?

- Is it dissonant?
- Does this composer write brief character pieces or long-form structures (or both)?
- Are the phrases long or is the music fragmented?
- Is it repetitive? Predictable? Repetitive? (Did you know I would do that?)
- Are there surprises?
- Are the endings formulaic, using standard cadences?

Ask yourself similar questions *as you compose* in the style of your nonexistent composer. Ideally, write more than one piece in this manner so that you can establish the style clearly.

BE A PRIVATE EAR

For the Chamber Music Society of Lincoln Center, I created the character Inspector Pulse, the world's greatest and only private ear, an investigator of musical mysteries.

For this exercise, you will be a private ear investigating a piece of music in order to figure out who the composer is. How do you go about it? You need a checklist to help you hunt for clues systematically.

Below is a list a private ear can use to check for clues to the mystery composer's identity. Choose a piece of music to investigate (or someone can choose it for you and hide the composer's identity) and use the list below to solve the case!

The checklist is not a definitive list of all characteristics of compositional styles. Rather, it is a guide to help focus analytical listening skills. Feel free to modify the list in any way that helps!

The checklist can be used in two ways:

1. Listen to a piece (and perhaps follow the score) *knowing* the composer's identity and check off characteristics on the list as you hear them. This is to form a sense of the composer's style so the list will be helpful later.

2. Listen to a piece when you do not know the identity of the composer and use the checklist to help solve the mystery.

PRIVATE EAR CHECKLIST

Texture

a. *Dense, concentrated*
b. *Clear, transparent*
c. *Focuses on low register, middle register, high register, or a mix of registers*
d. *Contrapuntal (polyphonic)*
e. *Homophonic (block movement)*
f. *Some independence of voices (but not strictly contrapuntal)*
g. *Use of sustain pedal on piano (essential to the music or not?)*

Rhythm

a. *Rhythmic unison (voices move together, as in homophony)*
b. *Regular meter, steady pulse*
c. *No steady pulse*
d. *Repetitive rhythm*
e. *Varied rhythm*
f. *Irregular accents*
g. *Time signature: standard/unusual*
h. *Shifting meters*
i. *Simple harmonic rhythm (rate of chord changes, if applicable)*
j. *Varied, complex harmonic rhythm*
k. *Polyrhythms (2 against 3, etc.)*
l. *Dramatic use of silence*
m. *Hardly any rests except at cadences or between sections*
n. *Rhythmic complexity in general*
o. *Dance rhythms*

Melody

a. *Lyrical, song-like*
b. *Motivic, mostly in short phrases*
c. *Interrupted phrases*
d. *Jagged, large intervals*
e. *Tonal, with some large intervals*
f. *Tonal, mostly diatonic*
g. *Tonal, modulates*
h. *Tonal, chromatic*
i. *Modal*
j. *Mix of modes (polymodal)*
k. *Folk music (or world music)—inspired*
l. *Whole tone*
m. *Octatonic*
n. *Invented mode*
o. *Atonal*
p. *Serial organization (12-tone, etc.)*
q. *Use of inversion, retrograde, retrograde inversion*
r. *Florid, with ornamentation*
s. *Repetitive*
t. *Form is simple (ABA)*
u. *Form is complex, organic*
v. *Virtuosic, instrumental, not singable*
w. *Octave shifts (displaced) common*

Harmony

a. *Tonal, mostly diatonic*
b. *Tonal, stable but chromatic*
c. *Tonal, modulates frequently*
d. *Tonal but unstable, highly chromatic moment to moment*
e. *Enharmonic modulations*
f. *Important bass line (guides harmony)*
g. *Sudden, unprepared key changes*

h. *Use of standard/traditional chord progressions (i.e., circle of fifths)*
i. *Triadic with some 7th chords*
j. *Triadic, 7th chords, 9th chords, 11th and 13th chords*
k. *Not triadic, chords formed by other intervals: clusters (seconds); quartal harmony (fourths)*
l. *Bitonality*
m. *Modal with triadic harmonies*
n. *Modal with chromatic harmony*
o. *Modal with clusters and/or quartal harmony*
p. *Polymodal (mixes or changes modes)*
q. *Polymodal chromaticism (mixes or changes modes and so generates chromaticism)*
r. *Octatonic*
s. *Whole tone harmony*
t. *Parallel harmony*
u. *Atonal (not in a key or mode)*
v. *Atonal, mildly dissonant, hints at tonality*
w. *Atonal, dissonant, no references to tonal harmony*

Dynamics
a. *Few dynamics notated in score*
b. *Some dynamics notated in score*
c. *Many dynamics notated in score*
d. *Sudden, unexpected, dramatic use of dynamics*
e. *Dynamics are integral/essential to the musical ideas*
f. *Extreme range of dynamics*

Cadences
a. *Traditional tonal cadences (authentic, deceptive, plagal, etc.)*
b. *Preference for certain cadences (i.e., plagal, chromatic)*
c. *Traditional tonal cadences with expanded or enriched harmonies*

    d. *Substitution of different harmonies for traditional tonal cadences*

    e. *Modal cadences*

    f. *Endings are not derived from traditional cadences*

    g. *Cadences from a non-Classical tradition*

    h. *Cadences from pop styles (fading out, ornamental flourish with some dissonances over a sustained chord, etc.)*

Of course, a private ear would also consider the *overall* style that the music suggests: Medieval, Renaissance, Baroque, Classical, Romantic, Expressionistic, Impressionistic, Neoclassical, Neoromantic, Jazz, Folk, Rock, Pop, Hip-Hop, etc.

Here are some examples of how to use the checklist to determine a composer's identity:

Characteristics	Possible Composers
• Transparent texture	Mozart, Haydn, Debussy, Ravel
• Homophonic, some contrapuntal	Beethoven, Schumann, Brahms
• Significant use of pedal	Chopin, Debussy, Messiaen
• Use of block rhythms	Handel, Beethoven
• Steady pulse, standard meter	Bach, Handel, Haydn, Mozart, Beethoven, Schubert
• Lyrical	Mozart, Chopin, Mendelssohn, Fauré
• Modal/tonal, polymodal, octatonic, whole tones	Debussy, Ravel, Stravinsky, Janacek, Bartok, Britten
• Modal cadences	Fauré, Debussy, Ravel
• Virtuosic piano writing	Chopin, Liszt, Ravel, Scriabin, Rachmaninoff, Messiaen

Characteristics	Possible Composers
• Parallel harmony	Satie, Debussy, Ravel
• Substitution of different harmonies for traditional cadences	Poulenc, Ravel, Prokofieff
• Dense texture	Brahms, Berg, Rachmaninoff
• Focuses on low register	Brahms, Prokofieff
• Polyrhythms frequent, some shifting accents	Brahms, Stravinsky, Bartok, Prokofieff, Carter
• Regular meter/pulse with cross-rhythms and over the bar syncopations	Schumann, Brahms, Stravinsky
• Varied harmonic rhythm	Schumann, Brahms, Janacek, Stravinsky
• Tonal, stable but chromatic, enharmonic modulation	Schubert, Liszt, Brahms, Fauré
• Preference for plagal cadences	Brahms
• Solid bassline guides harmony	Bach, Beethoven, Brahms, Fauré
• Shifting meters	Bartok, Stravinsky, Prokofieff, Copland
• Varied accents	Schumann, Brahms, Shostakovich
• Invented modes	Bartok, Britten, Shostakovich
• Clusters	Cowell, Bartok
• Chromatic, triadic	Chopin, Liszt, Schumann, Brahms, Strauss
• Folk music inspired	Haydn, Stravinsky, Kodaly, Bartok
• Inversions, retrogrades	Schoenberg, Webern, Stravinsky

Characteristics	Possible Composers
• Canons	Bach, Bartok, Stravinsky, Schoenberg, Webern, Hindemith
• Sudden, unexpected use of dynamics	Beethoven
• Dance rhythms	Bach, Haydn, Mozart, Chopin, Ravel
• Bitonality, bitonal harmonies	Ravel, Bartok, Prokofieff, Britten, Poulenc
• Triadic harmony, also chords by other intervals (fourths, fifths)	Hindemith, Copland
• Clear, transparent textures	Scarlatti, Haydn, Satie, Ravel
• Octave displacements are common	Stravinsky, Copland

Once you have become familiar with the checklist and are comfortable using it, you are ready to be a private ear.

COMPOSE A PIANO PUZZLER

Select a simple, well-known melody (it may be best to use a short tune like *London Bridge Is Falling Down* to start with). Select a composer whose music you know well and reimagine the tune in that style. Be sure to refer to the checklist as you work and ask yourself about texture, rhythm, melody, harmony, dynamics, and cadences. After you complete a first draft, use the checklist again to see if you used everything as you intended. If something is missing or unclear, fix it!

When you have polished the piece, play it for friends to see if they can guess the composer's style.

Isn't it amazing that when we listen to music and can identify the composer or the style, we are actually hearing the musical characteristics on that checklist and—consciously or unconsciously—putting it all together?

We take in much more information than we can deconstruct, analyze, or itemize unless we make a serious effort. By using a checklist like the one above, we can enhance our analytical listening skills. As those skills become second nature, we will perceive more and more detail as we listen. The details enhance our memories. Memory serves the imagination.

CODA

This book is now concluding, but what is on my mind is how to keep it going. As with any creation—composition, musical improvisation, comedy improv, poem, essay, novel, script, or book of imagination exercises—the question of how to keep it going arises throughout the process. And as I mention in various ways throughout this book, possibilities for prolongation may be thought in of terms of *action*. A new phrase might interrupt, confront, contradict, affirm, deceive, surprise, enhance, intensify, simplify, disintegrate, or expand.

As in improv comedy, one could keep ideas going by thinking, "Yes, and . . ." or, as in a dramatic narrative, one might think "no, but. . .". And it is usually good to wonder, "What if?"

In closing, I hope this book opens some musical doors. Finally, let these exercises be a beginning. In conclusion, remember, as it says in many technology manuals: "Press any key to start."

> *When I examine myself and my method of thought, I come to the conclusion that the gift of imagination has meant more to me than my talent for absorbing knowledge.*
> —ALBERT EINSTEIN

ABOUT THE AUTHOR

Composer, author, teacher, and inter-disciplinary thinker **Bruce Adolphe** has spent decades helping people to hear and enjoy music in extraordinary ways. He is the author of several books, including *What to Listen for in the World* (1998), *Of Mozart, Parrots, and Cherry Blossoms in the Wind* (1999), and the chapter "The Musical Imagination: Mystery and Method in Musical Composition" in *Secrets of Creativity: What Neuroscience, the Arts, and Our Minds Reveal* (2019). Widely known for his weekly Piano Puzzler segment, broadcast since 2002, on public radio's *Performance Today*, Mr. Adolphe has been resident lecturer and director of family concerts for the Chamber Music Society of Lincoln Center in New York since 1992. Mr. Adolphe is also the artistic director of the Off the Hook Arts Festival in Colorado and has twice been a participant in the Salzburg Global Seminar. He is a composer of international renown, whose works have been performed by Itzhak Perlman, Yo-Yo Ma, Daniel Hope, Joshua Bell, Fabio Luisi, Angel Blue, the Brentano Quartet, the Metropolitan Opera Guild, the Washington National Opera, and over 60 symphony orchestras worldwide. He lives in New York with his wife, pianist Marija Stroke, their daughter, Katja Stroke-Adolphe, and Polly Rhythm, the opera-singing parrot.

INDEX

For the benefit of digital users, indexed terms that span two pages (e.g., 52–53) may, on occasion, appear on only one of those pages.

Figures are indicated by f following the page number

Printed in the USA/Agawam, MA
March 4, 2022

789953.007

En Kijivo la etoso estis streĉita jam antaŭ la unua raŭndo en la 31-a de oktobro. Proksimume 100 000 subtenantoj de la opozicio protestis ekster la elekta aŭtoritato, postulante justan kaj ĝustan kalkuladon de la voĉoj. Kaj tri tagojn antaŭ la voĉdonado Vladimir Putin ja vizitis Kijivon, por soleni sur la Placo de Sendependo la liberigon de Ukrainio el la nazia okupacio, kune kun Janukoviĉ. Ne eblis dubi, kiu estis la faborata kandidato de Rusio.

Juŝĉenko gajnis la unuan raŭndon kun marĝeno de iom pli ol duona procentaĵo. Enketoj ĉe la balotejoj indikis, ke li gajnos ankaŭ la duan raŭndon la 21-an de novembro. Tamen la oficiala rezulto anstataŭe donis klaran majoritaton al Janukoviĉ. Vladimir Putin gratulis sian ŝatatan kandidaton jam antaŭ ol la oficiala rezulto pretis, kaj Janukoviĉ elpaŝis en televido kiel gajninto, sed tuj estiĝis fortaj suspektoj pri elekta fraŭdo.

Observantoj de Organizaĵo pri Sekureco kaj Kunlaboro en Eŭropo rapide konstatis, ke okazis grandskalaj misagoj dum la elekta kampanjo, dum la voĉdona procedo kaj la kalkulado de la voĉoj. EU kaj Usono rifuzis rekoni la rezulton. Ĉiuj EU-landoj revokis siajn ambasadorojn de Kijivo proteste kontraŭ la elekta fraŭdo. Sur la Placo de Sendependo, kie Putin ĵus solenis la liberigon de Ukrainio el nazioj, komencis kolektiĝi grandaj kvantoj de protestantoj.

La kampanja aparato de Janukoviĉ asertis, ke la protestantoj estas direktataj el eksterlando, ke oni disdonis drogumitajn oranĝojn al la manifestaciantoj, kaj ke ĉion regas ekstremaj naciistoj – aŭ "banderaistoj", kiel oni ilin nomis en la rusia propagando, laŭ la naciisma gvidanto Stepan Bandera.

Tuj post la dua raŭndo Serhij estis invitita al Kijivo por partopreni defendon de doktoriĝa disertaĵo. Liaj kolegoj en la elekta stabejo de Janukoviĉ diris ke li ne veturu, ĉar estus tro danĝere en la ĉefurbo.

– Ili diris, ke tie estas "banderaistoj", ili vere tion kredis. Sed mi tamen veturis, kaj kiam mi venis al Kijivo, mi vidis la oranĝkoloran maron, ĉiujn, kiuj venis por defendi la elekton. Ĉio estis trankvila kaj paca. Kiam mi revenis hejmen, mi diris, ke mi ne plu volas